—The Story of—
An American Family

By
Susan Billings

Susan Billings
2015

—The Story of—
An American Family

By
Susan Billings

Etcetera Publishing LLC | Fort Worth, Texas
www.GenealogyBookPublisher.com

The Story of An American Family
Copyright © 2015 by Susan Billings

All rights reserved. No part of this publication may be reproduced, distributed, or transmitted in any form or by any means, including photocopying, recording, or other electronic or mechanical methods, without the prior written permission of the publisher, except in the case of brief quotations embodied in critical reviews and certain other noncommercial uses permitted by copyright law.

In no event shall the author or publisher be held liable for any special, incidental, direct, indirect, exemplary, or consequential damages of any kind, or any damages whatsoever, including, without limitation, those resulting from loss of use, data or profits, whether or not advised of the possibility of damage, and on any theory of liability whether in an action of contract, tort or otherwise, arising out of or in connection with the use or performance of the information in this publication or its related links or on any other basis.

The text contained within this publication is
for information purposes only.

ISBN 978-0-9899112-7-6

Published by:

Etcetera Publishing LLC | Fort Worth, Texas
www.GenealogyBookPublisher.com

Cover and Interior Design by Sheila Fredrickson

Table of Contents

To My Grandchildren vii

Acknowledgments ix

Family History Timeline xi

Ancestors xiii

The Story of An American Family xv

ONE: The Family's Beginning 1

TWO: From Dean Castle to Aghadowey 13

THREE: Londonderry 17

FOUR: A New Life in the New World 27

FIVE: Drums of Revolution 41

SIX: Challenges and Rewards in the New United States 51

SEVEN: On the Move Again 63

EIGHT: Grace Boies Chamberlain 87

NINE: Out of Cortland 115

TEN: The Post-War Years & Cultural Change 131

ELEVEN: A New Generation in Vermont................................. 139

TWELVE: A New Century, Weddings & Babies...................... 147

Family Photo Gallery 157

Family Letters 169

Family Obituaries 175

Bibliography... 183

To My Grandchildren ...

When I was young, I knew nothing about my family's heritage. I thought we were just Americans. But, as the computer made genealogy research so much easier in the early 2000's, I started looking. At first I was hoping to amuse my elderly mother, whom some of you remember as "Noni". In her late eighties and early nineties, she had gone almost blind, she couldn't walk well, her husband and all her friends had died, and she was the last left in her family of origin.

She had a large collection of family photos, newspaper clippings, and written memoirs, but couldn't see or read, so she liked me to read them to her and describe the pictures. Among these was an account written in 1884 or so, by Grace Chamberlain Walrad, my great-grandmother (you can figure out how she was related to you). It told the story of her own mother's ox wagon trek with her family from western Massachusetts to central New York State in 1812, when the mother, Samantha Boies Chamberlain, was a little girl of 6.

This story inspired me to look back further, to find out where Samantha came from, her father, her father's mother, and on and on, back further and further. Happily, there was a wealth of material about our family.

What I found was a story of America which is common to many families, yet extraordinary in its scope and range. It has nobles and paupers, danger in battle and on the high seas, heartbreak, loss, and great love.

I was able to go back almost 450 years, to 16th century Scotland, where our family was close to King James VI, follow them to the Irish Plantation, and from there across the ocean to America where they were penniless pioneers. They were people of toughness and grit, hardworking and thrifty, and unwavering believers in the Christian God. I chose one representative of each generation in our direct line, either a man or a woman, found out all I could about the people's lives, tried to fit them into their own historical context, and to imagine what might have been going through their heads as they faced so many inevitable challenges.

There have been fourteen generations from Jean Kerr to your generation, and each of you is a blood descendant of all of these amazing people. I hope you enjoy the story!

Susan Billings
2014

Acknowledgements

I would like to express my thanks to friends and relations for their encouragement in the completion of this project; especially to the five perfect grandchildren who inspired me just by being born.

Grace Boies Chamberlain Walrad really got the project going by writing down (in 1883) the story of her own mother's trek from Massachusetts to New York State in an ox wagon in 1812, when her mother, Samantha, was a little girl of six. Thanks also to my late uncle **Frank McKee,** who rediscovered, preserved, and passed along that story in addition to his collection of family obituaries, news clippings, and his excellent genealogy of the McKee family.

My late mother, **Jean Chamberlain McKee Hamacher,** saved and toted around countless family photographs, diaries, letters, memorabilia, china and silver and linen through many, many moves around the country. That these have all come down to me is a minor miracle.

I'm also grateful to **Rosalind Bond** for editing and instruction, and her 29th Street writing class at Austin's Lamar Senior Activity Center for support and genuine encouragement.

Paid membership in *Ancestry.com* has connected me with other amateur genealogists who are pursuing the some of the same family lines as I. The generous sharing of pictures, stories, and other genealogical information and sources has been invaluable.

More than ever, I admire the American system of public libraries and the fine people who run them. It seems one can go anywhere in the United States and find a comprehensive section of local history just waiting on the shelves of the library. I would especially thank the Mary J. Barnett Memorial Library in Guthrie Center IA, the Iowa Genealogy Center in Des Moines, the Cortland Free Library in Cortland, NY, the Worcester Public Library in Massachusetts, the American Antiquarian Society in Worcester, MA, the Leach Library in Londonderry, NH, the New Hampshire Historical Society in Concord, NH, the Griswold Memorial Library in Colrain, MA, and, most of all, the Porter Memorial Library in Blandford, MA, where I spent days of very worthwhile research.

The Cortland Historical Society, its very capable director, Mindy Leisenring, and her assistant Tabitha Scoville, graciously helped me with access to dozens of family archives, letters, wills, bills of sale, diaries, all of which gave me a richer sense of the real lives of our ancestors. Mindy also put me in touch with Homer's historian Martin Sweeney, who arranged for me to see and photograph the portrait of Rufus Boies at Homer High School.

And final thanks to Sheila Fredrickson, who, with knowledge and experience, helped me shape my work into something permanent, readable, and worth passing down to even more generations of this American family.

Family History Timeline

1594	Jean Kerr marries Robert Boyd
1596	James Boyd born—West Scottish Lowlands
1637	James Boyd marries Catherine Creyke of Yorkshire
1644	Rachel Boyd born in Aghadowey, Northern Ireland
1660	Rachel marries James Blair
1683	Robert Blair born in Ireland
1689	Siege of Londonderry
1703	Robert Blair marries Isabella Rankin
1718	Voyage to America, landing in Boston, August 4
1720	Robert Blair II born, Rutland, Massachusetts Colony
1746	Robert Blair II marries Hannah Thompson
1752	Dorothy (Dolly) Blair born, MA
1770	Trek to Blandford, Massachusetts
1772	Dolly Blair marries David Boies, Blandford, MA
1775	American Revolution begins
1777	Rufus Boies born, Blandford
1799	Rufus Boies marries Nancy Gibbs, Blandford
1806	Samantha Boies born, Blandford
1812	Trek to Homer, New York
1834	Samantha Boies marries Alfred Chamberlain, Homer, NY
1847	Grace Boies Chamberlain born, Homer, NY
1861	Civil War begins
1878	Grace Chamberlain marries Calvin P. Walrad
1880	Grace Catherine Walrad born, Cortland, NY
1908	Grace C. Walrad marries Frank W. McKee, Cortland
1917	United States enters WWI
1919	Jean Chamberlain McKee born, Beaver, PA

1923	Family moves back to Cortland, NY
1941	US enters WWII
1942	Jean McKee marries Howard Franklin Hamacher, Cortland
1944	Susan Chamberlain Hamacher born, Boston, MA
1969	Susan Hamacher marries Henry Frank Billings, Lexington, MA
1974	Miles Walker Billings born, Brattleboro, VT
1975	Jean Churchill Billings born, Brattleboro, VT
1977	Susan and Henry Billings divorce
2004	Miles Billings marries Felicity Smith, Brattleboro, VT
2005	Jean Billings marries Rene Omar Sanchez, Austin, TX
2005	Cesar X. Sanchez born, Austin, TX
2006	Keenan Wells Billings born, Baltimore, MD
2008	Graciela Susana Sanchez born, Austin, TX
2009	Eli McKee Billings born, Boston, MA
2009	Alejandro Anselmo Sanchez born, Austin, TX

Ancestors

1. Jean Kerr (b. 1577)   m.   Robert, the "Master of Boyd"
2. James Boyd (b. 1596)   m.   Catherine Creyke
3. Rachel Boyd (b. 1644)   m.   James Blair
4. Robert Blair (b. 1683)   m.   Isabella Rankin
5. Robert Blair 11 (b. 1720)   m.   Mary Hamilton
6. Dolly Blair (b. 1750)   m.   David Boies
7. Rufus Boies (b. 1777)   m.   Nancy Gibbs
8. Samantha Boies (b. 1806)   m.   Alfred L. Chamberlain
9. Grace B. Chamberlain (b. 1847)   m.   Calvin P. Walrad
10. Grace K. Walrad (b. 1880)   m.   Frank W. McKee
11. Jean C. McKee (b. 1919)   m.   Howard F. Hamacher
12. Susan C. Hamacher (b. 1944)   m.   Henry F. Billings
    - A. Miles W. Billings (b. 1974)   m.   Felicity Smith
    - B. Jean C. Billings (b. 1975)   m.   Rene Sanchez

The Story of
AN AMERICAN FAMILY

As all humans did, we came out of Africa about 60,000 years ago. Through the millennia, the people migrated generation after generation to the north, then east and west. They tamed animals, planted crops. They organized themselves into groups with different jobs. Then they started thinking about the past and the future and learned how to write things down. That's how we know when one part of our family started in the Scottish Lowlands, Lothian, near what was already the great city of Edinburgh four hundred and fifty years ago.

— CHAPTER 1 —
The Family's Beginning

Sometime in the fourteenth century the Kerr clan (whose name comes from the Old Norse *kjrr* or marsh dweller) brought their Viking blood across the Channel from Normandy to make their living on horseback by rieving and raiding cattle along the Scottish border with England. However, by the late 16th century, the Kerrs had long renounced their marauding and thieving family history and settled into Protestant respectability in southeastern Scotland. The family had accumulated enough political prestige and property to earn a barony, the barony of Newbattle[1] and in 1606 Mark Kerr was named the Earl of Lothian. His wife's name was Margaret Maxwell.

In 1595, they had arranged for their fifteen-year-old-daughter Jean to be joined in marriage to Robert, the Master of Boyd. This meant her moving west from the rough coastline of Lothian to the Boyd's ancestral home, Dean Castle, in Kilmarnock south of Glasgow.

---

1   Roddy Martine, Scottish Clan and Family Names (Edinburgh, Scotland: Bartholomew & Son, 1987), p. 121.

Robert Boyd's ancestors were native Scots, probably from the tribes of the Angles or Picts. Ironically, the very first Boyds had earned their wealth and political prominence fighting Scandinavian Viking invaders like the original Kerrs. The Boyd surname might have come from the island of Bute, which is directly off the western Scottish coast,[2] or it may refer to the hair color of Robert, an early family leader. *Buidhe* is the Gaelic for yellow.

By 1263, the Boyds were well established in Ayrshire, on the southwestern mainland of Scotland, where King Alexander III's goal was to rid the offshore islands of Viking settlement and influence. The ferocious Vikings, led by King Hakon, were eyeing the Firth of Clyde as their next invasion target. It came to a head on October 2, 1263, when the awesome Viking force of 120 ships and 20,000 fighters was anchored behind the islands off the coast of Largs, a regality where the Boyds were vassals. A fierce October storm came up and drove several ships ashore. After the weather cleared, a small group of Norwegians came in to salvage what they could, when they were attacked by a local force of Scotsmen armed at first with bows and arrows, slings and rocks.

As the word went out to both the Norse and Scottish camps and the battle grew in size and violence, both Kings Hakon and Alexander III were on the field, but as darkness fell, it ended indecisively.[3] After this battle, the Norse withdrew and the disputed islands reverted to Scottish sovereignty.

The legend depicted in the family shield of the Boyds is the hand of King Alexander III, who apparently needed to be somewhere else, saluting the brave fighter Robert Boyd with two fingers, and handing the conclusion of the Battle of Largs over to him with the word, "Confido", or "I have confidence that you can do the job!"

---

2   Gary, the estimable guide at Dean Castle, Kilmarnock.
3   Wikipedia.

— Susan Billings —

Family Shield of the Boyds

— The Story of An American Family —

Portencross Castle

Afterward, Boyd was awarded land and a title at Portencross, further south on the coast, where his mission was to continue defending the Firth of Clyde for Scotland. The castle is still standing on the western coast, now mostly in ruin.

At seventeen years, Jean Kerr Boyd had her first baby, a boy, whom they named Robert after his father, and when she was nineteen in 1596, her second son was born. His name was James Boyd, and he became our ancestor.

James grew up strong and sturdy. His older brother lived to be only thirty, and on the brother's death, James became the ninth Scottish Lord Boyd of Kilmarnock and inherited his father's castle and estates. He was one of the young nobles chosen by King James VI of Great Britain to receive a grant of 3000 acres of good land in Aghadowey, a small village on the River Bann in County Antrim, Northern Ireland.

King James VI of Scotland and James I of Great Britain, as a boy.

— The Story of An American Family —

River Bann

The King wanted a trustworthy group of English-speaking Protestants to sail the over-twenty-mile strait from Scotland, toss out the Irish Catholic landowners (many Irish had already been massacred), and establish a robust British settlement in Northern Ireland.

> The early negotiations and preparations were drafted by the London Livery Companies and in 1610 lands confiscated from the native Irish were planted by settlers from lowland Scotland. They had to work "with the sworde in one hand and the Axe in t'other."[4]

---

[4] Northern Ireland Tourist Board publication.

Our ancestor James brought 48 musket-armed workers over to Ireland after 1624. Of these, 20 had wives and children. Most were his own tenants from Kilmarnock.

The Scottish peasants were likely relieved to leave their rocky homeland for a slightly easier life in Ireland. Back in Scotland, most lived in hovels of piled stone with their animals at one end, and family at the other, burning peat or turf vented through a hole in the roof; vermin abounded in these rough shelters. Famine and diseases like smallpox, plague, rheumatism and skin infection were constant threats; life expectancy was 35. They didn't know how to drain the bogs, so mosquitoes proliferated along with malaria.

Since there were no fences, livestock had to be herded by children at all times to keep them out of the fields, where some of the soil was so poor that oats would yield only three seeds for one sown. A normal diet consisted of oatmeal, oatcake, pot herbs from the yard, beer and ale.

At the end of a winter, cattle were like skeletons. The people had to "lift" them out to the new grass, and "lifting day" was noted each year. Even in summer, the cows only gave about a pint of milk a day.[5]

In Ireland, James Boyd had his workers build homes—a manor house for himself and his future family, and modest shelters for the workers' families inside the manor walls. They put up fences and planted thick hedge all around the 3000 acres for big flocks of sheep and small herds of cattle. They broke open the untilled earth to plant barley and oats for their bread, and sowed fields of flax for their spinning wheels and looms.

In 1637, when Lord James Boyd was satisfied with the progress on his new Irish estate, he sailed back to Scotland to find a wife, but he found her in Yorkshire, northern England, right up against the

---

[5] James G. Leyburn, The Scotch-Irish: a Social History (Chapel Hill, University of North Carolina Press, 1962).

Boyd shield at Dean Castle

Scottish border. She was Catherine Creyke, daughter of a prominent family who claimed descent from the royal Plantagenets. James and Catherine spent their early married life at the Boyd family's Dean Castle near Kilmarnock, Scotland, the lands of which had been awarded in 1316 by Robert the Bruce, to the son of the first Robert Boyd, also named Robert Boyd, after his service as an important Scottish commander in the Battle of Bannockburn. Our ancestor Lord James Boyd established a school in Kilmarnock for the village and tenant children.

Dean Castle had a large banquet hall on the first floor, where guests would eat and sleep; overlooking the hall was a "minstrel's gallery" for traveling entertainers. The "Solar" up the stone staircase was where the Lord and Lady and their children stayed. The Keep also included an underground dungeon where unfortunate

Floor grate over the vertical dungeon hole

prisoners would be thrown down through a hole in the stone floor. Prisoners rarely, if ever, came out alive. The chamber was shaped like a square bottle with the only opening at the top, no doors or windows.

The Dean Castle has been restored and is now a museum open to the public near Kilmarnock.

SCOTLAND

ENGLAND

WALES

IRELAND AND THE UNITED KINGDOM

11

— The Story of An American Family —

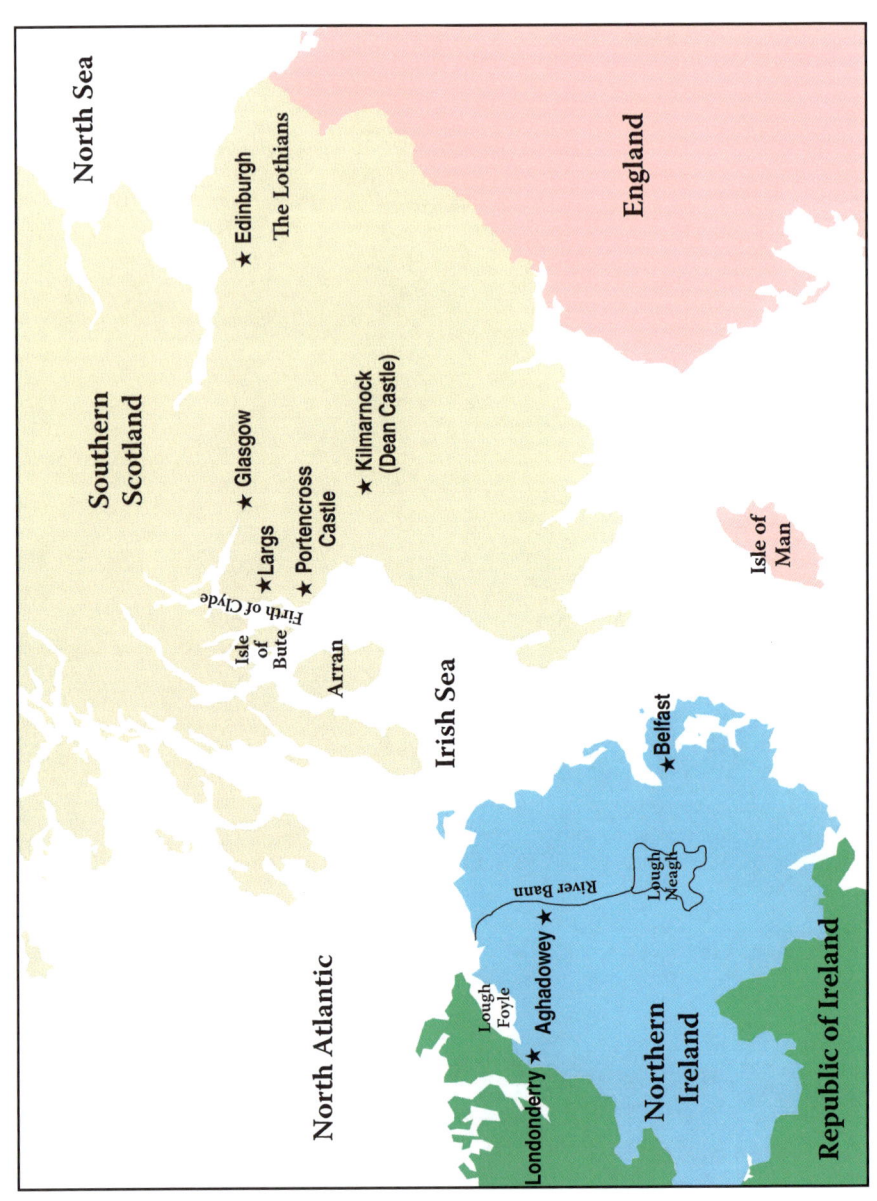

IRELAND AND THE UNITED KINGDOM

— Chapter 2 —
From Dean Castle to Aghadowey

James and Catherine often traveled back and forth between their estates in Scotland and Ireland, but five out of their six children, one boy and five girls, were born at Dean Castle, which Catherine probably thought was more civilized than Ireland. The sixth, their last baby, was a little girl named Rachel. She was born in 1644, (exactly three hundred years before your grandmother) in their new home in Aghadowey along the River Bann, and she was our ancestor.

Rachel Boyd loved growing up in beautiful green Ireland. A later visitor to Aghadowey (pronounced "Ockadooey") wrote,

> My eyes never rested on a lovelier spot. The silvery waves of the pastoral Bann kiss the shore as it winds its course towards its ocean home in the broad Atlantic. The country is

Dean Castle, Kilmarnock, Scotland (Thanks to Wikipedia)

well wooded and highly cultivated. No matter how humble the home, there is always a wealth of flowers around the dwelling. The cotters plainly have a great love of fruit and flowers, and not a foot of soil is left unfilled.[6]

As the youngest child in the family, Rachel might not have been as closely watched as the others, but she was still dressed in iron corsets as a five-year-old. Parents then thought the girls would grow up to be more graceful if they were confined as little ones. I hope Rachel had a chance to stretch her legs, run across the fields and wade in the streams when the elders were not looking.

While Rachel was a little child, her father James Lord Boyd was still travelling often back to Scotland and England. He was a curly-wigged cavalier active in the English Civil War in the service of King Charles I against the Puritans and Oliver Cromwell, and

---

6 Miss Mary Semple, 1890, quoted in Emily Wilder Leavitt, The Blair Family of New England (Boston, David Clapp & Sons, 1900), p. 20.

he was beginning to move away from the Anglican Church of the British nobility, closer to the Presbyterian faith of his fellow Scots in Northern Ireland. When forces of Oliver Cromwell were victorious (they even beheaded King Charles), Rachel's father James Boyd knew things were not going to go well for the Scottish landowners in Northern Ireland.

Despite her family's wealth and her own status as the lord's littlest daughter, Rachel experienced sorrow in her childhood. Her mother Catherine Creyke died when Rachel was 6, and her father James Boyd left her an orphan when he died four years later. It was probably her older brother who arranged her marriage, when she was 16 years old, to James Blair, an Aghadowey neighbor from the same Scots-Irish background.

James Blair was a Presbyterian, and sealed Rachel's commitment to that faith. They lived in a house where parts of the walls were six feet thick; some writers think it may have once doubled as a fort. The Blairs farmed in Aghadowey for many childless years of marriage until Rachel finally gave birth to twin boys in 1682 at the advanced age of 38. Their names were William and John. The next year, 1683, came Robert Blair, our ancestor, and two years later, Rachel and James' last son, Abraham, named for a brother of James'.

James Blair and his brother Abraham grew flax in partnership on their land in Aghadowey. They had a bleaching green called Ballywitt where great webs of brownish linen fiber whitened in the sun. The Blair brothers employed local workers to spread the webs on the green grass, some who spun and wove linen in their own homes, and others to prepare the textile for export through the port of Belfast.

— The Story of An American Family —

A Bleaching Green from the Hincks Engravings

— CHAPTER 3 —
Londonderry

During the time of Rachel's marriage, the English crown was making life more and more difficult for the Scots in Ireland. As "dissenting" Christians, they were allowed to follow their Presbyterian form of worship, yet were required to tithe ten percent of their income to the Church of England. How they could plant their fields was determined by the English market; if England wanted more beef, the Irish could use their pastures only for grazing cattle, not to plant oats or barley for their own bread. All the land was leased from the Crown and not owned individually.

Also, in Ireland, the Scots were surrounded by Irish Catholics, who viewed the Scots as religious heretics, and were resentful of their success. The seething Irish anger was liable to erupt into violence at any time. There had been a massacre of about 10,000 Scots-Irish by the native Irish in October, 1641, a few years before Rachel was born. On the 13th of December, 1641, a large army of Irish slaughtered the Scots who were settled at Garvagh. When the nearby settlement of Aghadowey heard about the disaster, they fled to safety in Coleraine, returning home afterward only to find their houses burned by the Irish. The surviving Scots settlers had been wary of their Irish neighbors ever since, though according to William Lecky, a 19th century historian, "it is far from clear on which side the balance of cruelty rests."

An anonymous note surfaced in Londonderry in late 1688, threatening another massacre of Protestants to match that of 1641. The rumor (which was later proved false), spread through the Scots-Irish communities causing about 30,000 panicked citizens of the surrounding countryside to pour into the walled city of Londonderry for safety.

On top of all these worries, in late 1688 King James II was deposed in England because he wanted to restore Catholicism as the state religion; the British Parliament invited Mary, James II's daughter and her husband, William of Orange, staunch Protestants, to come from Holland and take the throne. James II and his Jacobite army (supplemented with French forces) launched an invasion of Ireland on March 12, 1689, hoping to inspire the Irish Catholics to support his cause and restore a Catholic monarchy. The rebellious Jacobins worked their way from south to north Ireland. By the 18th of April, 1689, their army, which included King James II himself, stood at the Bishop's Gate right by St. Columb's Cathedral Church demanding entry to the walled city of Londonderry. The deposed King James himself hammered on the Bishop's Gate of the walled city expecting an immediate surrender, and he was astonished when the citizens fired on him from atop the wall.

Lieutenant Colonel Robert Lundy, the appointed Governor, was about to surrender, when a brave Protestant group of 13 teen-aged apprentice boys slammed down the Ferryquay gate, seized the keys to the city, hauled up the drawbridges, and locked all four gates of the walled city. Governor Lundy is said to have skulked away that night disguised as a peddler by climbing over the city wall and down a pear tree.

Rachel's husband, James Blair, rushed from Aghadowey to Londonderry in its defense, and may have remained there for the entire siege which lasted for three and a half months. His brother Abraham did stay. Total harmony didn't reign inside the walls; there were some religious quarrels among the different Protestants which the clergymen tried to soften. A few insiders snuck out of the walls to approach the Jacobites hoping to trade intelligence for food. This meant the defenders had to keep moving the dwindling supplies of armaments around in the city while it was continuously being pummeled with bombs lobbed over the wall by catapults.

Bombs muddied up the water supply. Thousands died of disease and starvation. The people were eating the leaves and roots of trees, salted horse hide, and the tallow of their candles which they spiced with herbs and called "French Butter". Through all this, an edict prohibited any speech of surrender.

The brutal French General Conrad de Rosen was summoned by King James and arrived at the River Foyle on June 18, 1689. He

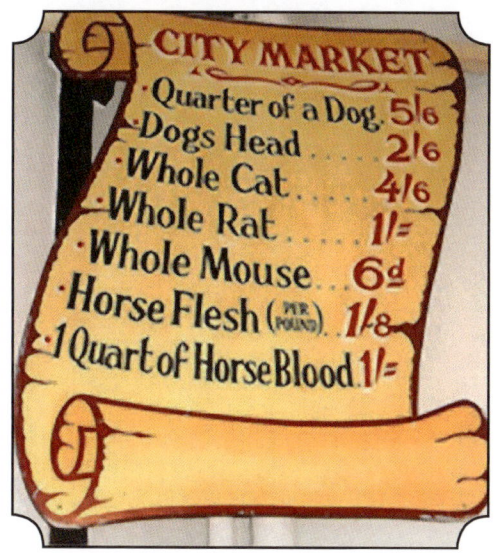

A grisly menu from the Siege Museum

ordered all the Protestant women and children of the surrounding countryside to be brought by force to the foot of the Londonderry walls. If the defenders still refused to surrender, the 4000 hostages would be put to the sword. The women prisoners begged the defenders not to give in. On July 4, de Rosen received a directive from King James II himself ordering him to desist in this brutal, unmanly tactic, and the hostages were freed, though hundreds died at the wall and on the way home.[7]

Forty miles southeast, in the normally peaceful village of Aghadowey, as de Rosen's soldiers attacked the helpless wives and children of the Londonderry defenders, Rachel Boyd Blair saw the Jacobins coming, and bolted with her four little boys to hide under the hedges that bordered the family's fields. The King's soldiers looted, and then destroyed their home. Watching it all from their hiding place was our five-year-old ancestor Robert. He was old enough to remember the scene the rest of his life; the wanton and cruel devastation of his home, also the despair and bravery of his beloved mother.

Finally the English ships Montjoy and Phoenix entered Londonderry at the River Foyle and chopped through the wooden boom barrier the Jacobins had floated and secured across the river. On July 28, 1689, Rev. McGregor of Aghadowey is said to have, as a youth, discharged the large guns from the tower of the cathedral which announced to the starving people besieged below that the ships were approaching up the Foyle to bring them relief.[8]

---

7 *History of Londonderry* [NH], Rev Edward Parker, orig. pub. Perkins & Whipple, Boston, 1851, new edition pb. Town of Londonderry, NH, 1974.
8 Rev. A. L. Perry, Professor of History and Politics, Williams College, *The Scotch-Irish in New England,* taken from *The Scotch-Irish in America: Proceedings and Addresses of the Second Congress at Pittsburgh* (Pennsylvania, May 29–June 1, 1890), p. 13.

The Phoenix was loaded with six or eight hundred barrels of meal whilst the Montjoy brought beef, flower and biscuit from England. 'This relief', says Walker [Rev. George Walker, one of the defenders] 'arrived here to the inexpressible joy and transport of our distressed garrison, for we had only counted on two more days of life.' [9]

That night the surviving population of the city saw hundreds of small fires all around the walls of Londonderry. After 105 days of siege, James II's army were burning their camps and marching away in defeat.

About a week later, the city came together for a Thanksgiving Service held in St. Columb's on the 8th of August, 1689, a tradition which continues to this day. The April "Shutting of the Gates" and the July "Relief of Londonderry" have also been reenacted and celebrated annually through the centuries.

After the Siege of Londonderry was broken, James returned and the Blair family rebuilt their home and farm. They cared for the great flax webs whitening in the sun on the bleaching greens of their land, supervised the spinning and weaving of their flax into soft and pliable Irish linen, and sheared their sheep for wool. The family weren't British nobility any more. They had to work for their living, while the oppressive English law continued to limit the Irish markets for their linen and woven wool.

Every Sunday Sabbath James and Rachel walked the short distance with their boys to the beloved "kirk", where the Reverend James McGregor preached a gospel of Christian liberation. Thanks to both trans-Atlantic trade and Presbyterian missionary work in America, word was starting to trickle back to the Ulster Scots of much greater religious and economic freedom in the American

---

[9] Emily Wilder Leavitt, *The Blair Family of New England* (Boston, D. Clapp & Sons, 1900), p. 17.

colonies. The neighboring district Presbyterian minister Robert Holmes had hitched west-bound rides to the colonies on returning tobacco boats for several years. He reported to his fellow Irish Presbyterian clergy that the Massachusetts colony was eager for Protestant settlers, and would actually make grants of acreage in risky western Indian territory to brave pioneers who would clear and civilize the land.

Our courageous ancestor Rachel was not destined to see the New World. She died at age 56 in the new century, May 10, 1700. Her devoted husband James Blair, raised a gravestone for her, which is still there in Aghadowey. Queen Anne took the British throne in 1702, and, because they were "dissenters", the Irish Presbyterians lost almost all of the political advantages they had gained by their victory in Londonderry. The Test Act of 1704 declared Presbyterian marriages invalid, their chapels and schools were closed, and a Presbyterian could not hold any public office higher than constable.

Rachel's sons, young teenagers in 1700, had been devastated by her death, but they toiled on for almost fifteen more years; until a six-year drought ravaged Aghadowey from 1714–1719. The crops failed year after year; the workers were starving, sheep were stricken with "rot", smallpox broke out, there was no income. The English Parliament had passed the Woolens Act of 1699, limiting production in Ireland and forcing the sale of all Irish wool at a fixed price to English wholesalers. Rents were rising for all the tenant farmers because the English landowners demanded more profit while production was reduced by drought. The Presbyterian minister Reverend Robert Holmes stepped in again. He worked with the Reverend Mr. Boyd scouring Aghadowey with his petition to present to Samuel Shute, Provincial Governor of Massachusetts (which included Maine) and New Hampshire.

Reverend Boyd, who had not signed the petition himself, sailed to Boston with 319 signatures of Scots-Irish, including that of James Blair (he spelled it Bleair), who were ready and willing to emigrate; nine of the signers were ministers, and there were only 13 who were unable to write their own name. This petition is now in the custody of the Historical Society of New Hampshire. It is described in detail by the Reverend A. L. Perry, a history professor at Williams College, in an address he gave to the Colonial Society of Pennsylvania on June 1, 1890:

> As an assurance to the governor of the good faith and earnest resolve of those who sent him, Mr. Boyd brought an engrossed parchment twenty-eight inches square, containing the following memorial to his excellency, and the autograph names of the heads of the families proposing to emigrate: "We whose names are underwritten, inhabitants of ye North of Ireland, Doe in our own names, and in the names of many others, Our Neighbors, Gentlemen, Ministers, Farmers, and Tradesmen, Commissionate and appoint our trusty and well beloved friend, the Reverend Mr. William Boyd of Macasky, to His Excellency, the Right Honorable Collonel Samuel Suitte, Governour of New England, and to assure His Excellency of our sincere and hearty inclination to Transport ourselves to that very excellent and renowned Plantation upon our obtaining from His Excellency suitable incouragement. And further to act and Doe in our Names as his prudence shall direct. Given under our hands this 26th day of March, Anno Dom. 1718."

Three years after his mother's death, when he was 20, our ancestor Robert Blair had married his lovely neighbor Isabella Rankin, descended herself from a prominent Scots-Irish family near Londonderry. This young couple had none of James and Rachel's fertility problems. The babies came fast—Matthew in 1704, David in 1708, John in 1710, Dolly in 1711, Sarah in 1715. Our Robert, as well as his brothers and most of his neighbors, was determined to move the family to America. He worked toward that goal tirelessly as the babies arrived and his workforce and income suffered from drought and English economic oppression. Aghadowey's parish leader, the Reverend James McGregor explained the Presbyterians' motivation to emigrate:

> to avoid oppression and cruel bondage, to shun persecution and designed ruin…and to have an opportunity of worshipping God according to the dictates of conscience and the rules of His inspired Word.[10]

Isabella had recently had her sixth baby, a boy named William, when the large family attended their beloved kirk in Aghadowey for the last time, and heard the Rev. James McGregor preach his farewell sermon from Exodus 33:15. The passage records a conversation in the Sinai Desert between the Lord and Moses, who is leading the Israelites out of slavery in Egypt. Moses asks God, "If thy presence go not with me, carry us not up hence," and the Lord answers, assuring Moses that his tribe will be watched over.[11]

Along with almost all their neighbors, Robert and Isabella Blair boarded the two-masted brigantine *Robert* at Belfast for Boston in the late spring of 1718. They may have covered their passage by selling the few years remaining on the lease to their land. Of course, they carried with them their own hero of Londonderry,

---

[10] Patrick Griffin, *The People with No Name: Ireland's Ulster Scots, America's Scots Irish, and the Creation of a British Atlantic World 1689-1764* (Princeton, NJ: Princeton University Press, 2001), p. 90.
[11] Leavitt, op. cit., p. 24

Robert's father, James Blair, who was 78 at the time. An obelisk-shaped monument commemorating the siege still exists in the city of Londonderry, or Derry, as it is known now. It may bear the name of our ancestor, James Blair, but a good source says the list of names is limited to those who lost their lives in the Siege. Fortunately, James survived to immigrate to America.

The Blairs had sold their home, their farm with all its stock and outbuildings, and what household goods they could, but there were so many families migrating from Aghadowey at the time, it's hard to imagine they made much profit. They packed up their Bible, light tools, food, clothing and bedding for the journey. Isabella had to bid her parents goodbye, knowing they would never meet again.

The passage across the Atlantic must have been very difficult. The passengers and crew couldn't know how the wind would blow, or how many weeks they would be at sea. There was always the risk of infectious disease, or of food running out on the voyage. Besides her elderly father-in-law, Isabella had six children to look after in the small tossing ship; Matthew was 15, David, 11, John was nine,

A Brigantine

Dolly, eight, Sarah was three, and William was no more than a few months old. The weather was completely unpredictable in 1718; Captain James Ferguson of the *Robert* never would have known if a hurricane was blowing up from Africa. And there were pirates!

Yet the brigantine *Robert* was part of a fleet of five crossing the ocean that spring and summer, transporting about 120 Scotch-Irish economic and religious refugee families from Northern Ireland. She arrived safely at the little wharf at the foot of State Street in Boston on August 4. Considering the large number of persons in the average Scotch-Irish family, there were likely at least 750 people on board the five ships. The oldest was John Young at 95, and the youngest was probably ocean-born. Describing the Blair family perfectly, Mr. Griffin quoted a Philadelphia newspaper:

> most who arrived are Protestants, and principally Dissenters [Presbyterians], and such as are remarkable for their Knowledge in raising Flax, and all other Branches of Linnen Manufacture.[12]

---

12 Griffin, op. cit., 79, quoting the *Pennsylvania Gazette,* 12 June, 1735.

— CHAPTER 4 —
A New Life in the New World

Bostonians, who numbered about 12,000 in 1718, were amazed and a little alarmed at the size of the crowd of immigrants that summer. Colonists who were hoping to hire indentured servants were disappointed; thrifty as always, these Scotch-Irish had mostly not mortgaged their passage. Bostonian Thomas Lechmere wrote to his brother-in-law a week before our family's arrival, on July 28, 1718:

> Shipps are comeing in hourly, but no news; Irish familys enough; above 200 souls are come in allready, & many now hourly expected; so that I wish you were here; they are none to be sold, have all paid their passages sterling in Ireland; they come upon some encouragement to settle upon some unimproved Lands, upon what other Towns I know not.[13]

---

13 Charles Knowles Bolton, *Scotch-Irish Pioneers* (originally published in Boston, 1910; reprinted Baltimore, MD: Clearfield Company, Inc., 2001), p. 133.

— The Story of An American Family —

Cotton Mather

The "encouragement to settle upon some unimproved Lands" came from Governor Shute and notably from Cotton Mather, the great religious writer and leader in Boston. Mather was motivated by sympathy for his fellow Protestants suffering in the clutches of the English crown, but also by his vision for the development of the Colony of Massachusetts. His diary of September 20, 1706; "I wrote letters unto diverse persons of Honour both in Scotland and in England to procure Settlements of Good Scotch Colonies to the Northward of us."[14] He wanted these hard-working farmers to expand British settlement westward, to eliminate the Indian threat and establish an agricultural base sufficient to feed and clothe the growing colony.

---
14 Powers, Mary J., *The Blair Family of New England Revisited*, publisher; Mary J. Powers, Blandford, Massachusetts, 2008, p. 15.

Governor Shute was also anxious to move the five ship-loads of Scotch-Irish to the west and north in New England, "as a frontier-barrier against the French and Indians of Canada."[15]

The English and Puritan New Englanders were especially fascinated by the unique tools the Scotch-Irish had brought with them for the cultivation of flax and the manufacture of linen textile, a new industry to America. The women of our group actually presented a spinning and weaving exhibition at Boston Common in the spring of 1719, where prizes were awarded to the most skilled. If she could spare the time, Isabella might have participated in this contest. The first ladies of Boston rushed to take up spinning as a useful hobby, and during the next four years, they "paraded on the common to exhibit their newly-learned art, derived from their stalwart sisters from over the sea."[16]

The newcomers were close enough ethnically, linguistically, and religiously to the dominant culture in Massachusetts that they weren't actively persecuted in Boston. Indeed, Cotton Mather himself wrote to a friend in Scotland,

> We are comforted with great numbers of our oppressed brethren coming over from the North of Ireland unto us. That which adds very much to our comfort is that they find so very little difference in the management of our Churches from theirs and ours, as to count it next unto none at all. [They] sit down with us, and we embrace them as our most united brethren, and we are likely to be very happy in one another.[17]

Yet many established Bostonians were not keen on the rough and penniless Scotch-Irish sticking around the city for long. Lechmere

---
15 Perry, op. cit., p. 15.
16 Perry, op. cit., p. 18.
17 Griffin, op. cit., pp. 90-91.

complained that "these confounded Irish will eat us all up, provisions being most extravagantly dear, and scarce of all sorts."[18] Even the tolerant Cotton Mather soon changed his opinion:

> [the Ulster Presbyterians have] been a marvelous grief unto us...[and] that among our United Brethren who have lately come from Ireland unto us...there have been some who have most indecently and ingratefully given much disturbance to the peace of our churches."[19]

The Robert and Isabella Blair family may have had a plan, or they may have had to wait until their arrival in the New World to make contact with friends or relatives to help them get started on their new life. They left Boston quite soon, and may have worked for wages at farms in Sudbury, Rutland, Marlborough, and Worcester. Native Americans had been driven recently from this area 50 miles west of Boston; two earlier white settlements had been abandoned there due to Indian attacks, the first in 1675 during King Philip's war and another in Queen Anne's war in 1709.[20]

This group of about 50 new Scotch-Irish families more than doubled the population of English Puritan Worcester, which had established itself only five years previous. The English tolerated the newcomers for the first years of their association. They needed the Presbyterians to keep the town going. Reverend Perry describes the new arrivals:

> So far as their physical natures went, they had received in the old country a splendid outfit for the race of life, in large bones and strong teeth, and a digestive apparatus the envy

---

18 Ibid., p. 91.
19 Ibid.
20 Perry, op. cit., p. 3.

of the mountain bears. Men and women both were trained to an almost tireless physical industry.[21]

The Scotch-Irish introduced the potato to their new home town. It was a welcome addition to a "scant and poor" daily menu which relied on bean porridge, barley broth, hasty pudding (ground corn in milk), and samp (an Indian word for pounded corn porridge).[22] While they nurtured their fields, their flocks and herds, the settlers needed to depend upon bountiful game and fish for their protein.

---
21 Ibid., p. 18.
22 Ibid., p. 25.

In these first years, Worcester consisted mainly of five garrison houses, one of which was a block fort. Until they could procure their own land and cabin, our Blairs must have stayed each night together with many others in the garrison house, typically a bullet- and arrow-proof brick or stone structure with barricaded windows, gunslots, and a single narrow door that would only admit one at a time, the better to pick off any invading enemy. Robert was able to buy his own farm in Worcester on February 10, 1726, for 60 pounds, and built a house for his family which had enlarged from the six children they brought with them on the ship.

Our ancestor Robert II, the first of our family native to America, had been born in Rutland, Massachusetts, on June 10, 1720. An earlier immigrant, Cap't. William Blair owned the land that became Rutland; his relationship to this family is not clear. Little Robert's sisters Elizabeth and Mary arrived in 1723 and 1725, and the last of Robert and Isabella's 10 children, a boy named Joseph, was born in 1727. Their grandfather, James Blair, the widower of Rachel and hero of the Siege of Londonderry, lived until 1732 when he died at the remarkable age of 92, and is buried at Worcester. James' brother Abraham had settled for a time in Worcester, then bought property in Nutfield, another early Scotch-Irish settlement, which is now Londonderry, NH. The Reverend James McGregor, formerly minister at the parish of Aghadowey, also settled in Nutfield, and became known as the "Moses of the Scotch-Irish" for his great leadership in their migration. In gratitude for their service in the siege of Londonderry, the British government of the Colony of Massachusetts exempted brothers James and Abraham Blair and their descendants from taxation up until the American Revolution.

As the Indian menace abated, the English Puritans in Worcester grew less fond of their new neighbors. The Scotch-Irish had different habits of family life, cleanliness, alcohol use, language, and most especially, religion.

Even a formal act of the General Court of Massachusetts called them 'poor Irish people'...This designation they all naturally enough resented. 'We are surprised,' writes Rev. James McGregor, ...in a letter to Governor Shute, bearing date in 1720, 'to hear ourselves termed Irish people, when we so frequently ventured our all for the British crown and liberties against the Irish papists, and gave all tests of our loyalty which the government of Ireland required, and are always ready to do the same when required.'[23]

The English hired their own Puritan pastor, Rev. Isaac Burr, and taxed the Presbyterians to contribute to his salary and housing, promising that the Presbyterians could have their own pastor in the pulpit from time to time. But as time went on, and no Presbyterian clergy was approved to preach in the English meeting house, the Scotch-Irish withdrew from the Puritan Church and installed the Presbyterian Rev. William Johnston as their minister without a meeting house of their own in Worcester. A Scotch-Irish petition to the town for relief from the tax which supported the rival minister was answered with condescension:

> In answer to the petition of John Clark and others, praying to be released from paying toward the support of the Rev. Isaac Burr, pastor of the church in this town, or any other except Mr. Johnston, the town, upon mature consideration, think that the request is unreasonable, and that they ought not to comply with it, upon many considerations.

The summary of these "considerations" ends with this clear explication of the English belief that any difference in religious practice served only to weaken a given society:

---
23 Ibid., p. 4.

We look upon the petitioners and others breaking off from us as they have done, as being full of irregularity and disorder, not to mention that the ordination of their minister was disorderly, even with respect to the principles which they themselves pretend to act by, as well as with respect to us, to whom they stand related, and with whom they cohabit, and enjoy with us in common all proper social, civil and Christian right and privileges; their separating from us being contrary to the public establishment and laws of this Province; contrary to their own covenant with us, and unreasonably weakening to the town, whose numbers and dimensions will not admit of the honorable support of two ministers of the gospel, and tending to cause and cherish divisions and parties, greatly destructive to our civil and religious interests, and the peace, tranquility and happiness.[24]

As Robert and his large family worked the farm and got by through the 1730s and 40s, he became active in his Scotch-Irish community as a civic and religious leader. In 1732, he is recorded as "surveyor of the highways", and in 1735, he was on the committee to establish the Presbyterian meeting house where Mr. Johnston could preach in peace. A site was chosen close to the "Old Fort", where they had worshipped often. Because of their extreme poverty, it took the group five years to collect enough money for timber which the Presbyterian men, including Robert Blair (who had been appointed constable), and his older sons, raised and framed into the bones of their new church. In 1740, just as the building was beginning to take shape:

> ...the other inhabitants of Worcester, many of them persons of consideration and respectability and professed

---
24 Ibid., p. 6.

piety, gathered tumultuously in the night-time, leveled the structure with the ground, sawed the timbers, and burnt or carried off the pieces and other materials....The defenseless, but indignant strangers [the Presbyterians] were compelled to submit to this infamous wrong. The English Puritans and their irresponsible hangers-on chose indeed the night-time for their mob violence and devilish meanness, but no blackness of darkness can ever cover up a deed like this; no sophistries, no neighborhood mis-affinities, no town votes, no race jealousies...can ever wipe out that stain.[25]

This atrocity inspired many of the Scotch-Irish settlers to leave Worcester in disgust and establish their own towns further west in places like Western (now named Warren), Blandford, Pelham and Colrain. However, Robert (perhaps because of finances) stayed and continued his surveying work through the years, marking the boundaries of Worcester. In 1751, when he was 68, he deeded over his farm to Joseph, his youngest son, with the provision that Joseph support and care for his parents at their home during their lifetime. Isabella died first on February 10, 1765, at the age of 82. She is buried in Worcester, but an obituary has survived from the Philadelphia Gazette of May 2, 1765.

> "We hear from Worcester that lately died there, Mrs. Isabell Blair, aged 82 Years, formerly a noted Midwife in that Place. She hath left a Husband aged 81; eleven Children, ninety-three Grand Children, and twenty-two Great-Grandchildren; in all one hundred and twenty six. She lived with her Husband sixty-two Years, and during

---

[25] Ibid., p. 7.

— THE STORY OF AN AMERICAN FAMILY —

that time her own death was the only one that happened in the Family. She was decently interred in the new Mode."[26]

It is a tribute to Isabella's intelligence and skill as a midwife that her family was so successful. Midwives of the pre-revolutionary era not only delivered babies, but were also called upon to treat all sorts of ailments in their community.

Robert lived on after Isabella's death for almost 10 more years. He approached his father in longevity, passing at age 91, and is buried in Worcester also, under a stone with this inscription.

> In memory of Robert Blair who departed
> this life October ye 14, A.D. 1774.
> In the 91 year of his age.
> How great, how firm, how sacred all appears,
> How worthy an immortal round of years,
> Yet all must drop as Autumn's ripened grain,
> and earth and firmament be sought in vain.

At his death, he left six sons, four daughters, eighty-seven grandchildren, and one hundred and six great-grandchildren, a total of two hundred and three living descendants, all Americans. Apparently, one of the Blairs' sons and six of their grandchildren died in the ten years between Isabella's and Robert's deaths, but there were also eighty-four more descendants born.

Robert and Isabella's son Robert grew up right in the middle of the large Blair family. He listened to his grandfather James and the old man's stories of the Irish plantation, the brave and beautiful Rachel, the Siege of Londonderry, and the trans-Atlantic voyage, until James died when young Robert was a boy of 12. He had his hardworking Irish-born father as an example until our

---

[26] Powers, op. cit., p. 239.

American-born Robert was grandfather himself at 54. Young Robert may have had some informal schooling from his mother Isabella and father Robert. It was probably rudimentary arithmetic of the farm and market, and some reading from the Bible and Presbyterian tracts. Perhaps the ambitious senior Robert had persuaded another Scotch-Irish settler in Worcester to teach his children for a few years while they were still too young to be of much use on the farm. However he got his learning, Robert Blair became a man in the model of his father and grandfather.

As the immigrant father had established himself as a business, church and civic leader over many years of hard work in Worcester County, young Robert felt that American urge to seek his fortune further west. On April 2, 1746, at age 25, he married Hannah Thompson, a Worcester girl who had emigrated from Northern Ireland with her family only six years earlier. Their first child, another Robert, was born a year after their wedding on April 3, 1747, David followed in 1749, then Hannah, who did not survive her first year, and on December 9, 1752, Dorothy, always known as Dolly, who became our ancestor. These first four children were born in Worcester, where Robert was probably farming with his father, his father-in-law, or both. Robert is also called a "tailor" on some of his land deeds, so he must have had some training in that skill.

When Dolly was about three, the young couple made the risky decision to join a group of young Worcester families and move 24 miles west to Warren, Massachusetts, situated halfway between Worcester and the Connecticut River, a new town where Robert's older brother David had settled earlier. In 1755, Robert served for a short time in the French and Indian War at Crown Point, NY, and in August, 1757, he took part in the relief of the Garrison of Fort William Henry at the foot of Lake George, but escaped the massacre of the British by Native Americans. Robert may have taken or sent Hannah and the children back to the relative safety of Worcester during these military deployments.

Robert and Hannah had three more children while they were in Warren (at that time, the name of the town was Western; after the Revolution it was named Warren for the hero of Bunker Hill). Asa was born in 1756, Rufus in 1758, and another Hannah—at last a little sister for Dolly—on March 13, 1760. Because of the high childhood mortality rate, new babies of the same gender were often named for deceased siblings.

Dolly was well trained by her mother Hannah in the homemaking arts of the frontier. She might have attended a few lessons in a neighbor's home, but whenever she was needed for something at home, tending the younger children, cooking or cleaning, weeding or spinning, she could be called away from schooling.

After 10 years in Warren, the family was tempted by a land grant from the General Court of the Massachusetts Colony and also persuaded by Matthew Blair, Robert's oldest brother, to move farther west, to the Berkshire hill town of Blandford, where Matthew had been a pioneer. Early settlers had wanted to name the town "Glasgow" to remind them of their Scottish roots, and also because the people of Glasgow, Scotland, had promised the Americans a new church bell for the honor. The Colonial Governor, William Shirley, squashed their plan. He had just arrived from England on the ship *Blandford,* and wanted the new town named to honor his ocean passage.

The Robert Blair family had a hard trek across the Connecticut River and up the "Devil's Staircase", a steep, stumpy, rocky approach from the Westfield River up to the pioneer town of Blandford. Since the way was too rough for a wagon or cart, they were limited to what they could carry on horseback, even using their precious cows as pack animals.

On arrival in the Scotch-Irish town, Robert claimed his 500-acre tract called "the Gore", and he, with the help of several other men in the community, built the family a log cabin in the middle of unbroken forest. It was a low-ceilinged, one-room affair with a sole window covered in oiled paper. Heavy wooden shutters could be closed against the weather. The slab door was hung on wooden hinges or strips of hide. Furniture was primitive; split logs made their tables and benches, held together with wooden pegs.

When they weren't building, Robert and his older sons were hunting in the forest. The Scotch-Irish men were skilled with guns from boyhood; they killed deer, bears, squirrels, rabbits, wild ducks, and turkeys. The pioneers ate bear meat, but the fat or grease of the bear was its more valuable product, used in cooking, soap making, or mixed with healing herbs to make poultices for wounds. Its thick fur made a lovely rug before the fireplace.

> The ashes left from the burning of underbrush and tree trimmings, as well as ashes from fireplaces, were gathered for potash to be turned into lye for the making of soap. In the spring, the accumulation of wood ashes would be put into a barrel and water poured through the ashes. The brown liquid, or lye, which trickled out through a hole near the bottom, was then boiled in a large kettle with fats and grease saved from the winter's cooking. Several potash works were later established in the town which proved a great convenience to the women in the making of their soap.[27]

Hannah and the children were busy searching out wild fruits, especially the plentiful blueberries, and tiny wild grapes. Walnuts

---

[27] Betty E. Boies and Violet C. Wells, *The Descendants of David Boies of Blandford* (Massachusetts, R. E. Boies, copyright 1986), p. 34.

and hickory nuts added to their winter store. The Blandford women shared with Hannah their knowledge of teas made from sassafras, sage, and wild mint; also the medicinal uses of native herbs and roots. As they cleared the land for their spring garden, Hannah and the children piled up rocks on the side to save for fireplaces, chimneys, and walls.

They were a two-mile-long footpath away from the town fort, a risky journey that the family of eight needed to make every night through the wilderness for safety from frequent Indian attacks.

Early Scotch-Irish settlers in Blandford demolished several beaver dams, allowing plentiful grass to grow up in the resulting meadow. The next summer they would take a cow out to the spot, tie it to a tree, cut rows of hay with whittled sticks, feed the cow with cut grass, and refresh themselves from time to time with milk from the cow. When the men were working in the fields, they carried weapons and appointed one of their own as a sentinel. They were armed at all times, even in church.

Robert and his large family remained in Blandford for one or two years, then returned to Worcester. If his wife Hannah got tired of toting and herding the children to the fort every night, who could blame her for wanting to get back to civilization?

Since Dolly spent her years from age 13 to 18 in the more civilized city of Worcester, she probably had more educational and social opportunities than her older brothers, an advantage that would show up later when she raised her own children. But father Robert and his older sons loved the frontier and often traveled from Worcester back to Blandford to make improvements on their homestead. By 1769 or 70, the family was assured that the Indians had been driven out. Robert's entire family moved back to the rocky hilltop after five quiet years in Worcester. Robert and Hannah were now in their fifties.

— CHAPTER 5 —
Drums of Revolution

During these years British oppression was getting harder and harder for the colonists to bear. The yearning toward independence was growing in the hearts of Americans, especially in Massachusetts, and most especially with the Scotch-Irish, whose hatred of the English had been growing for centuries even before the early days of the Irish Plantation.

> The resentment which they carried with them continued to burn in their new homes; and, in the War of Independence, England had no fiercer enemies than the grandsons and great-grandsons of the Presbyterians who had held Ulster against Tyrconnell [at Londonderry and the Boyne].[28]

Some colonists, especially those of English descent, did not support independence. These Tories decamped to Canada and

---

[28] James Webb, *Born Fighting: How the Scots-Irish Shaped America*, (New York: Broadway Books, a division of Random House), 2004, quoting an English historian, James Anthony Froude, p. 153.

stayed loyal to the Crown, but the Scotch-Irish could barely wait to jump into the battle. "It would be the Scots-Irish who would bring the fire of revolution to the pulpits of almost every frontier church and also would provide a disproportionate share of guns and soldiers to the battlefield once war broke out."[29] Another history recounts: "In actual numbers this race of pioneers furnished about forty percent of the Revolutionary army, and an even larger percent of its fighting spirit.[30]

On April 20, 1775, the day after Paul Revere's midnight ride, Dolly's oldest brother, Robert III, answered the summons of the "alarm and muster" system, an east-to-west express rider network organized to deploy the citizen militia. His wife packed all the bread, salt meat, and old apples she could find in a sack as young Robert marched with Captain John Ferguson's regiment of 30 Blandford men, to join a company of Minutemen. To young Robert's dismay, they were too late for the battle, but they

> joined forces with a large number of other militiamen pursuing the British all the way back to Boston. The red coats of the British made them a good target for the Minutemen firing from behind fences and hedges, and from farmhouse windows. The finest British troops had been surrounded, ambushed, and outflanked, resulting in 273 casualties. This battle roused all America.[31]

This battle was the Redcoats' first experience with guerilla warfare. Robert's service lasted 18 days, including the regiment's long walk back home to Blandford from Lexington and Concord.

Another of Dolly's brothers, Rufus, was only 18 when he joined up as a private with Captain William Knox's Company, Colonel

---
29 Boies and Wells, op. cit., p. 34.
30 Ibid.
31 Ibid.

John Mosely's Regiment, and marched west from Blandford to Fort Ticonderoga on Lake Champlain on October 21, 1776 to reinforce the Continental Army that was holding Ticonderoga against the British marching down from Canada.

Back when the Blairs were settling once again into their Blandford cabin, Dolly, now a lovely, skilled and practical eighteen-year-old, was getting to know one of her family's neighbors, a young man named David Boies, whose background was very similar to hers. His parents were Scotch-Irish Presbyterians who had both been born in Northern Ireland. The first American Boies, a church deacon, arrived in Blandford around 1727, 40 years before the Blair family finally landed there for good. This earlier David Boies was a Blandford selectman from 1742–1752. He was rumored to be a descendant of the Huguenot noble Viscount DuBois who escaped to Scotland from religious persecution in France.

Young David's family wealth and property would have had a head start on Dolly's family, so, in the early 1770s, he was considered a good catch for the new-comer Blairs' eldest daughter. The couple were married by the Rev. Joseph Badger on December 1, 1772. Dolly turned 20 a week later on December 9, and David was 22. They settled near the Gore property of Dolly's father, Robert, off the Millard Road in Blandford.[32] Their babies started coming soon; William was first in 1773, Gardner in 1775, and their third son was our ancestor Rufus, born October 17, 1777.

That summer Dolly was caring for two-year-old William and one-year-old Gardner, and was pregnant with Rufus, when her husband David was drafted and marched west to Fort Ticonderoga. He left home on May 6, 1777, and returned July 14, 1777, a service of two months and seven days. Many of Blandford's men, including two of Dolly's brothers, volunteered or were drafted for short periods into the Revolution. The women of the town helped each

---

32 Powers, op. cit., p. 374.

Washing Clothes in the Stream

other to keep the gardens going, cutting hay and flax, and tending the livestock and slaughtering while their men were gone. They did this on top of their regular work of caring for the many children, cooking and baking, fetching firewood and water, spinning and weaving, candle and soap-making, and washing laundry in the stream.

Dolly's father Robert was 55 when the American Revolution broke out, too old for active service, but he supported the war effort from home with his usual boundless energy, serving on the Blandford Committee of Correspondence, Transportation, and Safety in 1775, 1776, 1777, and 1778. These committees, which existed in every small town, served to expand town meetings from purely local concerns to discussion of global politics and to stir people to collective action in support of the colonial forces; in general to champion the Patriot cause. Committee members organized and provided arms, powder, lead, and blankets to the continental army, they also scrutinized their townspeople for signs of disloyalty to the cause. They kept in close touch with a huge network of Committees of Correspondence from other little hill towns, Boston, and all the other American colonies.

David enlisted in the Continental Army for a second time on July 31, 1779, with Colonel Elisha Porter's Hampshire County Regiment, then was discharged to walk home one month later in New London, Connecticut. During this deployment Dolly had the three little boys and was pregnant with twins—girls named Dolly and Sophia, who were born in 1780.

Childbirth during these years was a difficult and dangerous experience. Sanitation was abysmal and the only anaesthesia available was alcohol, perhaps in the form of hard cider made from fall's apples by the groaning mother herself. Some mothers looked at childbirth as "the dreaded apperation", "the greatest of earthly miserys", or "that evel hour I loock forward to with dread."[33] The pangs of childbirth were considered God's punishment for Eve's disobedience in the Garden of Eden, and any expression of discomfort was firmly discouraged. Death of either mother or infant was not uncommon; indeed, the Reverend Cotton Mather, the Massachusetts minister who had encouraged the Scotch-Irish to immigrate, lost eight of his fifteen children before they reached the age of two.

The mother was attended by a midwife whose training came from apprenticeship and experience. Usually the mother's own mother, mother-in-law, and several female neighbors surrounded the bed to offer support and encouragement. No matter the season, after delivery these visitors kept a hot fire going, wrapped the new mother in blankets to help her sweat out "poisons", and brought in a large meal of several meats, meat pies, and tarts to rebuild her strength. Our Dolly must have been a very strong woman; she was pregnant most of her married life until her last baby was born when she was 43, and eleven of her twelve children survived to adulthood. Only the twin Sophia (b. 1780) didn't live past childhood.

---

[33] *Childbirth in Colonial America,* Digital History, University of Houston, www.uh.edu.

The women of Blandford supported each other through the war years in many ways. As patriots, they had long given up tea drinking; the product was imported and heavily taxed by the enemy British. Spinning and weaving their own linen and wool cloth was also an act of defiance against the British market. Their warm woolen blankets, knitted mittens and socks were critical equipment for the Colonial troops. The women turned the extra work into a social occasion with spinning, quilting and knitting bees held in one another's homes.

No Revolutionary War battles took place in Blandford, but military traffic came through the village. Soldiers with their equipment walked and rode from the east coast to battle sites at Lake Champlain, the Hudson River, or further west into New York. General Henry Knox, an Ulster Scot himself, was ordered by George Washington to take an expedition from Boston to the Forts Ticonderoga and Crown Point, arriving on December 6, 1775. They retrieved 60 tons of cannons and other artillery from the recently captured forts, hauled it all by ox-drawn sleds 300 miles back to Boston through Blandford. But before General Knox reached Blandford with his artillery train, some of the cannon crashed through the ice of a frozen pond in Alford, MA, near the New York line. (Divers recovered three of them in the early

2000s.) General Knox fit the wagon train through "the Narrows", a mountain gap west of Blandford by blasting out its jagged edges. The "terrible Glasgow Mountain" left a lasting impression on the General and his men.

It took the expedition six weeks, until January 27, 1776, but when the cannons were deployed at Boston Harbor (which the British had under siege), the enemy fleet was driven out and withdrew to Canada. General Knox went on to become George Washington's Secretary of War for the United States.

By custom, the men in expeditions like Knox's expected to receive food and shelter from the townspeople as they passed through. I imagine Dolly and David Boies were honored to host some of them. A later group did not meet the same welcome.

Mid-August of 1777, Blandford got the word that British general Burgoyne was marching down the Hudson from Canada and preparing to engage near Bennington. At sunset, another of our Blandford forefathers, Israel Gibbs, starting molding ball-shaped lead bullets in his home; by morning he had three or four hundred ready to go. He bagged up the bullets, shouldered his musket, and, along with several other townsmen, headed for battle. The men of Blandford arrived just as the Battle of Bennington ended in victory for the Colonial Army. While the regular soldiers rested from battle, Israel Gibbs and the other Blandfordites were assigned to guard the supplies and prisoners that had been captured from the enemy.

After the Blandford farmers returned home, the 700 British prisoners languished in Bennington for several months until Colonial officers finally got the order to march the prisoners, most of whom were German Hessian mercenaries, to Boston in early winter. As they followed the turnpike through Blandford, a severe snowstorm brought the group of POW's and their 1000 guards to a halt; food, shelter, and dry clothes needed to be requisitioned from the Blandfordites huddled in their homes. The prisoners were put in the church for the night, with Mr. Collester of Blandford in charge of the seven sergeants guarding the outside. Around midnight a loud crash sounded, the guards ran to the windows and, under orders, began to fire. Seven prisoners were killed and six wounded by the gunfire, but the morning light revealed what had really happened. The upper galleries of the church, stuffed with slumbering prisoners, had collapsed. Some were crushed and all were badly frightened. Mr. Collester forever regretted having given the order to fire on the desperate prisoners.[34]

Abundant crops of wheat had grown in Blandford before the Hessian POWs came to shelter in the church, but the next season was scanty. The belief was that the prisoners had brought the "Hessian fly" that attacked the corp. This may have been the first instance of an imported agricultural pest.[35]

On Friday, October 17, 1777, the very day that Dolly delivered her third son, our ancestor Rufus Boies, British Lieutenant General Burgoyne was in Saratoga, New York, surrendering to American Major General Horatio Gates after the Second Battle of Saratoga. Gates treated Burgoyne with respect, refusing to take his sword, and inviting him into a tent flying Betsy Ross's new United States flag to sign the formal surrender. It was a turning point in the War. The attempt to isolate New England from the southern states was defeated.

The next Sunday, Dolly and her new baby Rufus probably stayed home from the Presbyterian Meeting House, but her husband David, and Dolly's parents, Robert and Hannah Blair, were surely in attendance when word of the Colonists' triumph reached

---

34 Sumner Gilbert Wood, *Taverns and Turnpikes of Blandford 1733 – 1833*, (Blandford, MA, published by the author, Congregational Minister in Blandford, 1908,) p. 87.
35 Ibid., p. 89.

— Susan Billings —

General Burgoyne surrenders to General Horatio Gates at Saratoga

By John Trumbull, 1821
Original hanging in Rotunda of U.S. Capitol, Washington, D.C.

Blandford. In the Meeting House, Reverend Smith, according to a *Magazine of History* report,

> was trying to encourage his people toward a greater faith in God, that he would deliver though the thick darkness surrounded them. [There was] not a woman in that congregation who had not a husband, father or child present at the…battle. The text that Sabbath meeting was from the prophet Isaiah….'Watchman, tell us of the night? The watchman said, the morning cometh.' In his eloquence and enthusiasm, he [Rev. Smith] seemed to lift his hearers from gloom and despair to the height of God's promise and deliverance; 'We are now, even now, about to receive news of the fulfillment of God's promises. Amen! So be it!' as the words were spoken, and each one appeared as if in silent prayer, there came the sounds of flying hoofs; the steady beat came nearer, louder, as down the village street, to the church door, flew a foam-flecked horse and rider:…the rider leaped from the saddle…and strode up the main aisle; his armed heel rang as the blows of a hammer…Faces paled, and lips closed as in prayer.

A witness said, "As Dr. Smith reached forth to grasp the message, his hand trembled and an ashy pallor spread over his face. Tearing off the covering, the first words to meet his eye were, 'Burgoyne has surrendered!'"[36]

---

36 *Magazine of History,* quoted in Sumner Gilbert Wood, *Homes and Habits of Blandford, MA,* published by 250th Anniversary Committee, 1985, p. 91.

— CHAPTER 6 —

Challenges and Rewards In the New United States

The years just after the Revolution were not easy for the hill farmers. "An eloquent commentary on what war was doing in turning the countryside into a wilderness again, a committee was chosen to unite with neighboring towns to petition the General Court to help exterminate wolves, since too few men were left on the farms to clean out those skulking enemies."[37]

The Massachusetts government had borrowed large sums of money to finance the War, and, when it was over, taxes were raised across the board to pay off the debts. Men who had fought in the Continental Army had sometimes received no pay or benefits for their service, and the new American currency was very unstable for a period of time. The bankrupt State of Massachusetts levied higher and higher taxes on the farmers, taking them to court and confiscating property when the farmers could not pay. From

---
37 Ibid, p. 96.

August 29, 1786 to June 1787, Shays' Rebellion erupted as a local uprising of veteran farmers in western Massachusetts. Groups of protesters attacked and shut down courts in Northampton and across the state. During an attempt to take over the nearby Springfield Armory, four of Shays' rebels were killed. Blandford men were involved in the uprising, but no specific mention of any Blairs or Boieses is found. Shays' Rebellion is sometimes called the last battle of the Revolution. It served to aid the founding fathers in Philadelphia who were writing the new United States Constitution during the summer of 1787, reminding the writers that unreasonable tax burden and taxation without representation were some of the root causes of the War for Independence.

A contemporary portrait of Daniel Shays and Job Shattuck, leaders of Shay's Rebellion (Wikipedia)

Beyond his military service, Dolly's husband, David Boies, served his town and district in the years after the war as a town selectman, a moderator of town meetings, justice of the peace and a representative to the new legislature in Boston for 27 sessions from 1787, when he was still a young man of 37, until 1821, when he was 71 years old. David had a hand in making life easier in Blandford after the Revolution; roads and postal service were improved and market goods could get in and out. More of the town's children went to tax-supported schools.

Life for the former colonists, who were now citizens of the United States, was getting better. The families' focus moved beyond survival issues like getting enough to eat, taming the wilderness, and fighting the Indians, and toward a more settled and civilized way of life. Three of David and Dolly's sons went to Williams College in northwest Massachusetts. William Boies, their eldest, studied divinity and preached in Ohio; Joseph, their seventh child, became a lawyer and a judge in New York; and Artemus, the eleventh child, became a well-known minister who preached in South Carolina, Massachusetts, and Connecticut. Dolly never moved from Blandford in her adult life, but three of her sons had professional careers that untied them from the land and freed them to relocate.

Dolly's parents, Robert and Hannah Thompson Blair, lived close to Dolly in Blandford through the war years and the birth of the United States. The older generation helped their children and grandchildren in the house, with the babies, and on the farm, as the Dolly and David family helped the elders in their declining years. The 1790 census entry for the Robert Blair household indicates that another of Dolly's married siblings and their children shared a home with Robert and Hannah.

Robert and Hannah lived together into the new century. He died on June 22, 1801, at the age of 81, and is buried in the Old

Cemetery in Blandford. His stone, #58, is inscribed, "In memory of Deac'n Robert Blair who was born in Rutland June 1720 10th day & died in Blanford June 22nd 1801. Blefsed are the dead that die in the Lord."

Hannah followed him July 15, 1803 at age 81. Her stone, near to his, says; "In memory of Mrs. Hannah Blair who was the wife of Deac'n Robert Blair she departed this life July 15th 1 8 0 3 in the 81st year of her age". Low on the stone is written, "Mrs. Blair was born in Ireland." Both stones are topped with winged angel heads.

In that same first United States census in 1790, the entire Boies family is listed, but the only name on the census is father David's as the head of the household. Enumerated are five free white males under 16 years—Gardner, Rufus, son David, Joseph, and Lemuel. The two males 16 and over are father David, and first-born William, who was 17. The five free white females (not divided by age) are: Mother Dolly, daughters Dolly, Sophia, Cynthia, and Orpha. Their eleventh and twelfth children, sons Artemus and Justus, weren't born until after the 1790 census.

Dolly died on September 13, 1807, at 55 years old; six years after her father and only four years after her mother. Her youngest two sons were 12 and 14. She is buried in the Old Cemetery in Blandford. Dolly's stone is topped with the image of an urn and says, "In memory of Mrs. DOLLY BOIES. Wife of Cap't David Boies, who died Sept. 13, 1807 in the 55th year of her age. The flefh refts here till Jesus come And claims the treasure from the tomb."

Two years later, on September 24, 1809, David remarried a local woman, Clarissa Metcalf. Clarissa died in childbirth a year after the wedding, but David lived to the ripe old age of 89, passing on February 6, 1839, 31 years after his wife Dolly. Because of his years of service to the nation and the town, he is buried in the more prestigious Hill Cemetery in Blandford.

David and Dolly's third son, Rufus, born October 17, 1777, was our ancestor. Like your grandmother, he was born during a war, but his was the American Revolution. In his infancy, Rufus's mother Dolly probably followed the typical routine of colonial child care. Babies were often swaddled and spent most of their time in a father-built cradle. Sometimes the swaddled baby would even be hung up on the wall; everyone in the family was working too hard to be cuddling babies. Dolly would have nursed her babies for the convenience and safety of mother's milk. The richer urban mothers could hire a wet nurse, but Dolly might also have favored breast-feeding as a way to hold off the next pregnancy for a while.

When Rufus began walking, he was probably confined outdoors in warm weather with some sort of leash and no drawers to save washing the "clouts" and "pilcher" (a wool diaper cover) Dolly used. One-year-olds wore a padded "pudding cap" as they learned to walk. Not a bad idea! When Rufus was five or six, he was "breeched", that is, allowed to take off his baby gown and put on pants.

The children of Blandford didn't have much time for play. There were too many chores for boys, like chopping kindling, tending to livestock, weeding and gathering in the garden and orchard, picking sheep dung out of sheared fleece, and shooting and butchering game. When they could play, it might be a game of quoits (a rope circle thrown over a post), flying a kite, jumping rope, rolling a hoop, or tag.

Thanks to the efforts of his father and grandfather, there were three schoolhouses in Blandford during Rufus's childhood; a teacher was employed for three months a year, one month for each district. Today this doesn't sound like a lot of schooling, but it was better than nothing.

Because of his father's frequent absences with government duties, Rufus and his older and younger brothers grew up with a great deal of responsibility for supporting the family. His older brother William had gone to college at Williams, but Rufus's formal education ended at school in Blandford. He was 22 when he married Nancy Gibbs on the 5th of November, 1799. Nancy was 19, a descendant of one of Blandford's founding families, and one of seven children of Israel and Agness Clark Gibbs.

Rufus became a tavern- or innkeeper. Because of Blandford's situation on the east-west highway between Albany and Boston, the village enjoyed substantial traffic after the Revolution, and was able to support more than one tavern. Taverns and inns would supply food, drink, and lodging for travelers, and also for their horses. Roads were improved so much that there was even a scheduled stage service through the village. Inns were the social center of each town; church and government meetings would nearly always be adjourned to the local tavern after worship or business was done. Sermons were discussed and arguments hammered out at the tavern. The itinerant Yankee peddler would make the tavern his first stop. He might be offered some free refreshment in return for regional or national gossip and news.

Rufus's tavern was a frame building with a front porch, a far cry from his parents' log cabin. Blandford had progressed enough to support a sawmill, and the growing Boies family probably lived on the tavern's second floor.

In the very early 1800's, America had a powerful drinking habit. Water was considered unhealthful. The household cow's milk was most often preserved as butter or cheese. There was no refrigeration, so beer and hard cider, preserved by their alcohol content, were made at home and taken with every meal, even by children. Molasses for rum was imported from the West Indies. Whiskey was distilled at home from various grains. If you didn't want to run the "still yourself, it cost 50 cents a gallon with the jug thrown in."

"Flip" was a very popular drink in taverns and considered truly American. It was "made in a great pewter mug or earthen pitcher filled two-thirds full of…beer, sweetened with maple sugar, molasses, or dried pumpkin, and about [a pint] of New England rum was added. Into this mixture was thrust a red-hot poker which was always kept ready in the coals of the fireplace. The poker made the liquor bubble and foam and gave it the burnt, bitter taste the people seemed to like."[38]

Rufus did well in his business, earning himself the title of "squire." Nancy worked at preparing food with him at the tavern and was always busy with her growing brood. Their first-born, Dolly, named for Rufus's beloved mother, was born in 1800, then Leverett Gibbs Boies in 1803. Samantha, our ancestor, came on April 18, 1806. She was born during the administration of the third president of the United States, Thomas Jefferson, who had recently sent explorers Lewis and Clark out west to report back on the Louisiana Purchase. Israel, named for Nancy's father, arrived in 1808, and William in 1811.

In the early 1800s Blandford was experiencing some of the problems that happen when towns grow. Newcomers of English, African-American, and other ethnicities were moving in. The original Scotch-Irish population had been very clannish for generations; they voyaged to America together, and trekked further and further west together, and they didn't take kindly to new people in their town. The Presbyterians were becoming more

---

38 Boies and Wells, op. cit., p. 19.

— Susan Billings —

Thomas Jefferson
*Third President of the United States
By Rembrandt Peale, 1800*

isolated from their Presbyterial governing bodies, and it was harder and harder for the deacons to find a minister of Scotch-Irish descent. The younger members were willing to compromise enough to hire a Congregational pastor, but the older and more conservative factions could not agree.

Drunkenness was leading to family poverty and lawsuits, debt, and confiscation of property. Slavery was an important topic of moral discourse. As the economy and commerce improved, and American lives became less about endless drudgery, women began to wonder whether they might claim some of the human rights mentioned in the Declaration of Independence.

Perhaps as a reaction to these shifts in the old order of society, a religious revival later called the "Second Awakening" sprang up, not only in Blandford, but all across the brand-new country. Circuit riders offered camp revival meetings, with issues ranging from repentance of sins and conversion of the spirit, to women's suffrage, temperance, and abolition of slavery. Established church membership soared and entirely new denominations appeared, like Seventh Day Adventists, Disciples of Christ, the Church of Jesus Christ of Latter-day Saints (Mormons), Evangelical Christian Church, African Episcopal and African Methodist Episcopal Church.

Women and young people made up the majority of converts during the Second Awakening. They weren't in the pulpit, but behind the scenes organizing women's prayer groups, reform societies, and missionary guilds. One could imagine that if the common curse of drunkenness affected her home, an individual woman would find the temperance message very attractive. Religion gave the new American woman a social outlet and a purpose outside the home, where the relentless work had gotten a bit easier thanks to improved roads, and stage and postal service that brought some manufactured goods into Blandford.

Rev. John Keep at age 78
By Francis Bicknell Carpenter, 1859

A new, charismatic Congregational minister, John Keep, age 27, was called to the old Presbyterian Meeting House around 1808. He had traveled on the revival circuit, but had recently married and was content to settle in Blandford for a while. Keep was on fire with reform.

> When the time came for awakening upon the subject of temperance reform the church was prominent in it all. It was not afraid to go right into the broad aisle and rebuke the men of substance and dignity. And this it did. Rev. John Keep was a fearless and effective pioneer....It was high time for reform, not alone in Blandford, but in all the country. Too many boys were being drawn into the whirlpool.[39]

---

[39] Sumner Gilbert Wood, *Taverns and Turnpikes of Blandford 1733–1833*, (Blandford, MA, published by the author, Congregational Minister in Blandford, 1908,) p. 246.

Nancy was very enthusiastic about the religious revival and united in 1808 with the Blandford Congregational Church, pastored by John Keep. Rufus followed her in membership in 1811, the first of his family to break with the Presbyterian Church in over 125 years. One can imagine Rufus and Nancy absorbing Keep's temperance sermons and discussing their responsibility and their standing with God when it came to staying in the tavern business in Blandford.

A swinging Blandford tavern sign from 1795. Under the "Porter" name, you can see the name of Rufus Blair, Dolly's brother and Rufus Boies's uncle, an earlier tavern keeper. The sign is on display at Blandford's Porter Library.

CHAPTER 7
On the Move Again

Reverend Keep encouraged his followers to join him in a westward migration to Homer, New York, in the center of that state, near the glacial Finger Lakes. Keep had spent time there, perhaps in a church, or a traveling revival, and he saw it as a fresh start for the Scotch-Irish Blandfordites, who were drinking too much and getting crowded out by newcomers. In Homer, the farming was much better than in the rocky and stumpy Berkshires. A constant river ran through it and the fertile soil was easily plowed. Most of the Natives had already been driven out; there was a sawmill, a gristmill, and a shop, and plenty of virgin forest remained.

Rufus and Nancy must have turned the decision over and over in their minds, just as their own ancestors had struggled when they determined to come from Ireland to Massachusetts almost a hundred years earlier. In the same way as their ancestors, Rufus and Nancy had a large group of friends and relatives that were going west, and they urged the family to join them. Rufus's mother Dolly was gone, but a family move to Homer meant leaving behind his father David Boies, and both of Nancy's parents, Agness and Israel Gibbs. The couple must have prayed mightily on their decision.

The Boieses did what they felt they had to. In the next year, Rufus sold the tavern, most of his household furniture and tools, and all of his property except what could fit into a two-wheeled ox wagon. Again, since many in the village were leaving at once, he wouldn't have gotten a very good price. The night before their departure, Rufus, who was 35, and Nancy, 32, and their five little ones stayed with Nancy's parents, Agness and Israel Gibbs, because their home had been sold and any furniture they had left was dismantled and packed into the ox wagon. Dolly was twelve, Leverett, nine, our ancestor Samantha was a six-year-old, and her little brothers Israel and William were three and one.

We actually have Samantha's memory of this, recounted by her own daughter;

> Only a few months before her death, when almost eighty years old, she [Samantha] told about staying with her Grandmother the night before they started on this long journey and how she slept in the garret. It was quite an undertaking to leave home and old associations in those days, when journeys were only taken with an ox team.[40]

I imagine Samantha lying on a straw mattress in that attic, gazing at the moon outside the small window and wondering what the future held for her.

The Boies family and their large group of Scotch-Irish got on the road in the early summer of 1812. The community drove their ox wagons westward twelve or fifteen miles a day, and each child had his or her chores. When the wagons stopped they let the chickens out of their pens to feed, then cooped them up again for

---

40   Grace Boies Chamberlain Walrad, family papers, n.d.

the night. The young ones were up early each morning gathering fresh eggs or heading down to the stream for washing and cooking water. They loved berry picking, and there were probably plenty of sweet summer raspberries, scratchy blackberries, and blueberries all along their route.

Since the journey was just a matter of weeks, the families probably didn't need to supplement their barrels of salt meat by hunting, but nine-year-old Leverett might have enjoyed donating a fat river fish for the family supper. Nancy had a bowl of cornmeal soaking in water and salt most of the day, and at the fire each night she would fry up Johnny cakes with a little grease on her old iron spider. Big sister Dolly, who was 12, must have helped her mother Nancy with the cooking and washing, as Samantha kept her eye on the two little boys, William and Israel. As a three-year-old, William needed to ride in the wagon with baby Israel, while the rest of the family walked the distance or rode on the horse or cow tied to the wagon.

When they stopped for the night, there may have been music around the fire accompanied by a fiddle or banjo. "Oh, Where have you Been, Billy Boy?" and "Froggy Went a-Courting" were popular folk songs of the time. But the evening gathering always ended for the devout Scotch-Irish with hymns, Bible reading, and prayer. The Boieses' ox wagon, full of everything they could take from Blandford, would not have had sleeping room for the family of seven, so they pitched a tent, or slept under the stars, as the group's men shared sentry duty.

The road west had been improved during and after the Revolution. Travel was not difficult up, down and through the Berkshires. The ox carts had traveled forty miles from Blandford, fording several small streams and the Housatonic River when they left the Commonwealth of Massachusetts at the village of

Stockbridge and entered New York State. When Sunday arrived, the Presbyterians stopped for their Sabbath day of rest.

Two days after crossing the state line, they were traveling on the Rensselaer and Columbia Turnpike, a toll road, when they reached the Hudson River. The children must have been amazed at its size and the volume of flowing water. It's likely they stayed close to the path of present-day Rt. 90, and crossed the Hudson on a ferry just south of Albany at the village of Rensselaer. It must have taken at least a day for the large group of pioneers, their wagons and animals, to be hauled across the mighty river.

On the western side of the Hudson, they had a smooth shot to their destination of Homer over the rolling hills snuggled between New York's two important mountain ranges, the Catskills and the all-but-impassible Adirondacks. They traveled on what was then called the third Great Western Turnpike, another toll road, begun during the Revolution and completed in 1811, the year before the Blandfordites' trek. Today it is a two-lane freeway known as the Cherry Valley Turnpike or Route 20, but its current usefulness has been eclipsed by two great east-west Interstate Highways streaking across New York.

At a rate of fifteen miles of westward progress a day, the Boies family and their companions would have arrived in Homer just a week or ten days after crossing the Hudson.

It must have been joyous for the whole group to arrive at Homer and be greeted by old friends and earlier emigrants from Blandford. The family might have stayed with friends, or more likely, they set up their tent on the plot of land that father Rufus had chosen on the road west of Homer.

Rufus soon joined with the other men in the forest felling great trees to share for their log cabins. Rufus's crew worked on his own plot, and the Boies family was able to use the cleared and stumped land later for their pasture and cornfields. Rufus and Nancy had chosen a protected site on their land at the foot of a small hill. They planned their house facing east to catch the morning sun, close by a small stream for easy access to water until they could dig a well.

After the logs were cut, stripped of branches, and dragged to the building site by their faithful oxen, construction of the simple cabin only took two or three days. A stone foundation had been laid to raise the cabin from the damp earth. The logs, which were the same species for all four walls and the floor, were left with bark on to protect them from decay. The wall logs were squared off and notched at each end with the men's single tool, the axe. No nails were used—nails were too expensive to buy and too heavy to transport.

After the logs were piled in place with the aid of an ox-powered pulley system, the roof was laid with straight limbs cut from the felled trees, then covered with water-proof bark and thatch. Rufus and Nancy planned a loft under the roof, a place for the bigger children to sleep, and also for food storage. To support this extra half-floor, a couple of logs were laid across the empty space before the roof was constructed.

Rufus and his crew cut one door and one window, then it was the children's turn to chink the hundreds of small gaps between the horizontal logs, first with sticks and wood chunks, then animal hair, moss, and straw, and finishing with mud and wet clay. Dolly, who was 12, Leverett, nine, and six-year-old Samantha were eager to help, and they felt proud to be contributing to the family's new dwelling.

Before the family could reassemble and move all the furniture that was piled in their ox wagon into the new cabin, Rufus had to build a fireplace for cooking and warmth—the winter was coming on. The inside of the hearth, where Nancy would roast meat on a spit, hang her kettles of soups and stews, and fry up corn cakes, was built of stone set in clay. Nancy and the children had been collecting these stones from the nearby stream since the family arrived. Tireless Rufus built the chimney with more clay and mud shaped and strengthened with cut tree limbs. It was surprisingly fireproof. For their early fires, the family axed up sticks and tree limbs left over from building the log cabin.

The doorhole was draped with deerskin until a milled door could be hung, and the window was covered with paper smeared in pig fat, which made it both waterproof and translucent. Glass was rare and too expensive for the dark pioneer cabin.

The Boies family was delighted to light their first fire and freshen up the dampness of the new cabin, then set up their dear, familiar beds, tables, and chests, linens and clothing, plus Nancy's spinning wheel and loom, all brought so carefully over the two hundred miles from Blandford. When the chimney needed to be cleaned of built-up soot, Nancy would wait for a warm day, let the fire go out, and then Rufus or Leverett would climb onto the roof and drop a live chicken down the chimney. The flapping of its wings on the way down would sweep the chimney clean.

The family had basic shelter for the winter of 1812-1813, but Rufus and Nancy had higher ambitions for their home. In the spring, Rufus took advantage of the Homer sawmill, owned by a man named Rice, to construct both the loft floor, a door, and a framed room at the front of his log cabin, the first one built in Homer. Later exploration of these early Homer structures turned up pine and hemlock planks of 24 to 30 inches wide. These first white settlers were cutting virgin forest.

Here's a story of another early Homer family who settled just a few years after the Boieses:

> ...John S. Squires, took up a hundred acres of land...and built a log cabin to house his large family, a wife and twelve children, of whom James was the youngest. At the cabin door his wife hung a blanket until the time might come when her husband could make something more secure. The only windows were openings covered with oiled paper. One day when the children were playing in the clearing in front of the house, a big bear suddenly emerged from the woods and made for the baby James. The older children seized the child and rushed for the cabin. The bear retreated to the woods...[41]

Newly arrived Blandford farmers in Homer claimed their land in forested acreage, but the community had been formed for fifteen or so years, and it was relatively civilized, with a good east-west road, saw-mill, gristmill, store, tavern, schoolhouses, village

---

41 Bertha Eveleth Blodgett, *Stories of Cortland County* (Cortland, N. Y., Cortland, N. Y. Historical Society Publication, Frank Place, editor, 1952), p. 64.

green, and house of worship. The earlier settlers had also come from New England Scotch-Irish stock, so our family felt welcome and comforted.

There was even a newspaper! In 1813, it was called *The Cortland Repository*. The only relic Mrs. Blodgett could find for her 1932 history was from July 21, 1814:

> The reading matter of the paper is largely occupied with the closing days of the War of 1812. It gives one a peculiar feeling to note that a battle had been fought as near old Homer as Niagara Falls and that Indians played no small part in the forces of both the British and Americans. 'The Dethronement of Napoleon Bonaparte' also is of interest enough to occupy a column.[42]

Bertha Eveleth Blodgett penned her slim volume, *Stories of Cortland County*, in 1932, drawing heavily on the collections and stories of her father-in-law, Alonzo C. Blodgett, a member of the third generation of white settlers, who went on to live for 91 years.[43]

The Boieses had a small flock of chickens providing eggs for the family, a cow for milk and butter, a horse or two for transportation, their invaluable oxen, and a few sheep for wool and meat. After they packed up the eggs, and turned milk into butter in the wooden churn, Dolly and Leverett took what the family didn't need and sold it to their Homer neighbors. The money they earned was used at Jedediah Barber's new dry goods store in the village, to buy the few things they couldn't produce at home.

---

42 Ibid., p. 120.
43 Mrs. Blodgett enjoyed writing a local history column for the Cortland Standard and lectured extensively on Cortland County history for numerous clubs and organizations. As a personal friend of Grace Walrad McKee's, Mrs. Blodgett gave Gracie a copy of the second printing of the book in 1952, which has made its way to Susan's collection.

Calico was 25 cents a yard, way more than a thrifty homemaker like Nancy wanted to pay. She and the two girls spun flax and wool on the spinning wheel that had been brought from Blandford. Nancy had also brought her cumbersome family loom in the ox wagon, and after setting it up in the cabin, she wove great lengths of linen and flannel for the family's shirts, towels, and bed sheets. Flax grew well in Homer, and most families planted it in with their vegetables.

Getting the plants ready for the spinning wheel was a lengthy and difficult process, but the woven linen was so durable that it could last for several generations.

There were plenty of sheep in Homer, sheared annually to supply wool for the family's dresses and suits. Their blankets were quilts pieced together by hand from the rare clothing that wore out. The Boieses brought many of these quilts that had been handed down from their families back in Blandford. Nancy told the children stories of the patches and the memories they held for her.

In more settled and richer communities than Homer, there were itinerant weavers that would stay with the family, weaving the yarn that the women and children of the household had spun and dyed, and working on the family's loom until the weaving was done. But Nancy made her own fabric on her own loom.

In later years, Samantha told her daughter what happened when company came unexpectedly from a long distance to the cabin in Homer. It was so exciting for the family to have visitors, and the first thing her mother would do was to take down the loom and pack it away so as to have room for guests. She would go out and kill some chickens, dress them and cook a great supper for the hungry company. They would all sit down to a delicious meal of fried chicken, potatoes, cornbread and carrots at nine or ten at night, and about eleven the visitors would start off for their long ride home, thinking they had had a delightful time.[44]

Homer had its own town militia in the eighteen 'teens and twenties; Rufus and the other men drilled on Homer Green. Each September brought the day of "General Training", when all the militias of the surrounding towns would converge on the Homer Green to perform their drills before Major General Hathaway. Mason Loring, a young boy in those days, recalled his memories for Mrs. Blodgett:

> When we…heard the fife and drum on the Homer Green we couldn't wait to walk, but would run down the hill as fast as our feet would carry us.…We boys thought it a great honor to hold the horses while the officers dismounted.…The uniforms would be trimmed with gold lace. We could hardly contain ourselves when the regiment marched in review to the tunes of 'Bonaparte Crossing the Rhine' and 'Yankee Doodle'. A hollow square would be formed, and Reverend John Keep, [formerly of Blandford] for many years chaplain of the regiment, would offer prayer.[45]

---
44   Walrad, op. cit.
45   Blodgett, op. cit., p. 175.

The Boies family was keen on education for their children. In 1796, years before the family had moved from Massachusetts, the earliest white settlers of Homer had appropriated $40.78 for the establishment of a common school on the village green. Standards at that little school were not high. One teacher "advised his pupils to skip fractions, as they would probably never find any occasion in life when they would have to use them." Another Homer teacher "taught the children that the earth was round, explaining, however, that in so teaching he was following what the book said, although it was his personal opinion that the earth was flat.... The early school tax for each child was paid in wood."[46] A retired school teacher, T. Mason Loring, described the primary school experience:

> Children were sent to school very young. They were taught the A. B. C.'s first. They had the privilege of sitting on benches with no backs, their feet not reaching the floor. They had no books or slates with which to amuse themselves....The schoolhouses were made of logs and when the children could spell baker, baby, and cider, they were thought to be learning very fast....The teacher ruled, not with a rod of iron but with a rod of birch. I can remember how it felt as the teacher applied it to my shoulders, whipping out the dust from my roundabout [a short jacket] and coming right through to my skin. A good scholar was rarely punished, however. Sometimes the larger boys, partly to pay off the teacher and partly in fun, would go for him and put him out of the window.[47]

In 1818, when Samantha was 12, Rufus and several other town fathers raised funds and designed the Homer Academy, a high school which was incorporated by the New York State Board of

---
46   Ibid., p. 129.
47   Ibid., p. 128.

Regents and opened on February 2, 1819, housed at first in the Methodist church. Boys and girls came from all over New York State. They paid $5 a term in tuition, and boarded with local families for $1.50 a week. Samantha had had her early schooling at home with Nancy and Rufus, then became one of the first pupils at the Academy while it was still in the church. She became known for drawing very fine maps, and the principal of the school offered her one free term of high school tuition if she would leave her maps to be copied by future students. We don't have the maps, but the letter is on file at the Cortland Historical Society:

(Samantha's maps might have looked like these, which were drawn in Vermont, 1828, by a schoolgirl named Frances Henshaw, a little younger than Samantha. Maps courtesy of David Rumsfeld)

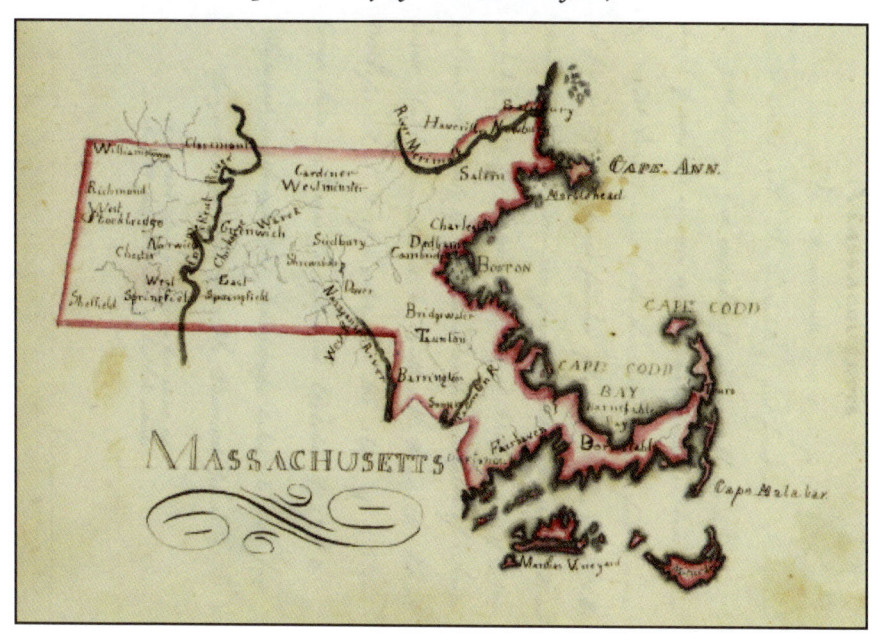

— The Story of An American Family —

Rufus Boies
By Francis Bicknell Carpenter, 1854

To Samantha Boies

My dear Miss B.
My negligence is unpardonable. I hope you will excuse it.
I want to propose that if you will come to school long enough to make another Chart, I will furnish you with paper and pay your tuition and [illegible]…none have made them much handsomer.

In great haste
C. A. Hale

Rufus Boies and the other original trustees of the Homer Academy (including the famous Reverend Keep), had their images immortalized by Francis Bicknell Carpenter, a Homer native, in a series done much later, in 1854. These oil portraits are still in possession of the Homer School District. Rufus also served the community as one of the founders of the Homer Agricultural Society, in 1838, he was treasurer, and in 1845 he was the president. The Agricultural Society held an annual fair with livestock, produce and cooking competitions, booths, and races each September. In 1830, along with his old friend Rev. John Keep, Rufus was a director of the Homer Bible Society which distributed relief funds and Bibles to the poor.

In 1820, when Samantha was fourteen and attending the Homer Academy, her adored older sister, Dolly, nineteen, was married at home to Stephen Russell and traveled west with her new husband to Lyme, Ohio. It must have been hard for their mother Nancy, to lose Dolly's capable help around the house. Rufus and Nancy had had another daughter, Nancy Clark Boies, their sixth child, in 1814, after settling in Homer. Little Nancy only lived to be six, she died the year of Dolly's wedding.

Dolly and Stephen's wedding trip from Homer, NY, to Lyme, Ohio, took thirty days over rough roads with all their household goods in a lumber wagon. Samantha's daughter wrote later that the newlyweds "must have had a great deal of love to have lasted them through such a journey."[48] Dolly had five children in all; unfortunately, she died when she was only 31.

During Dolly Russell's lifetime, father Rufus, who was postmaster of Homer by this time, allowed Dolly's younger sister and brother, Samantha, 20, and Leverett, 23, to make the journey to Lyme to visit the Russell family. Rufus drove them north in 1826, from Homer to the small village of Syracuse where the newly completed Erie Canal had opened the previous year. The brother and sister rode a canal barge towed by mule west to Buffalo, then boarded a sailing vessel on Lake Erie. Samantha's daughter wrote later that "when she [Samantha] was nearly to the end of her journey and was just thinking how glad she would be to be on land again, a wind came up and drove them back and it was three days before they were able to bring the boat to land! She was dreadfully seasick all the time."[49]

Dolly and her family came north from Lyme Township to meet Samantha and Leverett at the port of Sandusky, Ohio, west of Cleveland and south of Detroit. It must have been a joyous reunion, and Samantha would have been so glad, after the heartbreak of her little sister Nancy's early death, to meet Dolly's new baby daughter named Nancy. Samantha made three trips altogether from Homer to Ohio to see her sister Dolly, Dolly's husband Stephen, and their five children. The United States had experienced such rapid economic growth and improvement in commerce and transportation after the Revolution, that a pleasure trip for an average young woman like Samantha was newly possible.

---

48 Walrad, op. cit.
49 Ibid.

The Aqueduct Bridge for the Erie Canal across the Genesee River at Rochester. Woodcut, printed by Everard Peck, Rochester, about 1827.

It was during the 1820s, family legend has it, that Joseph Smith, founder of the Church of Jesus Christ of the Latter Day Saints, or the Mormons, came ambling up to Rufus one day, and announced "The Lord told me I was to borrow your mule today." Surely Rufus obliged.

Samantha enjoyed her school years and travels thoroughly, but after graduation from the Homer Academy, she felt the need to help her family and community. She taught in public school for several years, the first woman in the family to take paid work outside the home. One of her jobs was in Port Watson, a part of the present Cortland, NY, where there was a paper mill on the Tioghnioga River. This was a rough placement for Samantha because she had to board with the different mill families, some of whom were "not very agreeable. She was dreadfully homesick."[50] Samantha was getting more and more interested in the "boy next door", Alfred Chamberlain, the son of Charles Chamberlain who had the farm just south of Rufus Boies. The two young adults had always been friends, but now they had deeper feelings for one another.

---
50 Ibid.

Her younger brother Israel, who had been the baby in the ox wagon, married Mary Ives in 1833, and the newlyweds moved into the farm with their parents, Rufus and Nancy. Maybe the now-crowded house in Homer finally persuaded Samantha, at age 28, to accept her dear friend and neighbor's proposal of marriage.

Alfred Lyon Chamberlain had been born in Homer on November 5, 1805. He was less than a year older than Samantha. His parents were Deacon Charles Chamberlain and his wife Roxsey Lyon, who had been married in 1805 in Brimfield, MA, another town rich with Scotch-Irish history. Deacon Chamberlain had arrived in Homer in 1801. He bought 50 acres in the middle of Homer for $50 and soon donated 6 acres of it, a portion to the church, and some to the town for use as a village green (where Rufus drilled with the militia). Alfred, as the oldest child in the large family, "performed much of the arduous farm labor in his early life."[51] He was a serious boy, and very diligent about his education, enrolling in the Cortland Academy (Homer Academy was renamed after its county), where he and Samantha were classmates.

Samantha Boies and Alfred L. Chamberlain were married on April 23, 1834. She was 28 and he was 29, a rather older bride and groom than earlier generations of the family. After their wedding, Alfred and Samantha moved onto the farm Alfred had purchased on the Little York side of Homer.

Their little red farmhouse had just one room and a bedroom, but Samantha was happy to furnish a home of her own. "She had a very handsome set of china, white with a sprig on, that she bought herself."[52] Our family still has the teapot and creamer from this set.

Babies didn't come right away. The young couple moved after two years to another farm closer to Homer where all of their four girls were born. Caroline, named for her grandfather Deacon

---

[51] Henry Perry Smith, *History of Cortland County* (Syracuse, NY: D. Mason Publishers, 1885), p. 452.
[52] Walrad, op. cit.

Charles, came first in 1836, Sarah and Mary were twins born in 1842, and our ancestor Grace arrived in 1847, when Samantha was 41. Mary, one of the twins, died at 14 months of dropsy, or congestive heart failure, after having chicken pox. The family moved again in 1849, to a farm on the west road to Homer, where they stayed until 1884, by which time Samantha and Alfred were grandparents themselves.

Alfred Chamberlain was a very successful farmer, prominent in local agriculture. Merino sheep breeding was a keen interest, as was raising Durham cattle. The wool and meat he produced may have helped sustain Union troops during the Civil War.

Every Sabbath Alfred took Samantha and the girls to the Congregational church of Homer, which was united with the Presbyterian Society. Both Alfred and Samantha were faithful to the religion of their Scotch-Irish ancestors.

Alfred was public-spirited in many ways. He was a founder and long-time president of the Cortland County Agricultural Society, and served for years as a trustee on the board of Cortland Academy. He was always a stalwart of the Congregational Church, and a president of the Cemetery Association, doing much of the mowing and clipping himself to keep the Homer Cemetery beautiful.

Samantha and Alfred's daughters attended the Cortland Academy, which was at its most successful in the mid-century. It had excellent teachers, and many students came from far away to board in Homer and attend classes. The eldest daughter, Caroline, had had scarlet fever at six years old in 1842, the year the twins were born. It weakened her for years, her health failed when she was in her teens, and though she was a fine French scholar, she had to drop out of school and could not graduate. Caroline later contracted tuberculosis and died a spinster in 1872, when she was 36.

— The Story of An American Family —

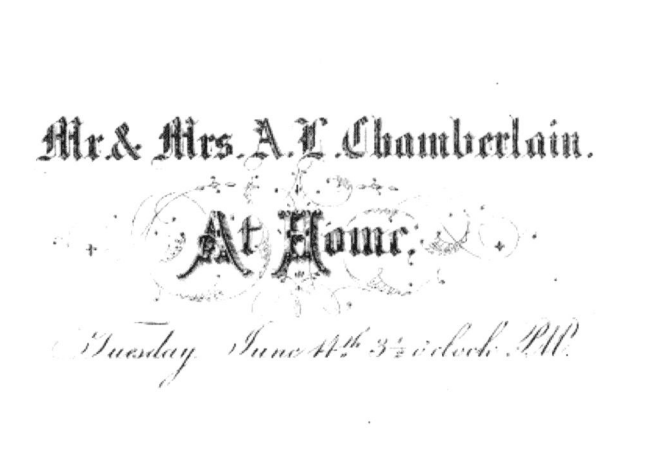

Alfred & Samantha's "At Home" card

The teapot and creamer from Samantha's set of china.

Sarah, the surviving twin, was, "a short, chubby, rosy-cheeked girl, a very fine student and a great favorite with her teachers. She graduated in both classical and scientific courses in Cortland Academy. She was exceedingly popular with all her schoolmates and always had a house full of company."[53] Sarah graduated from the Academy in the spring of 1861, when she was 19, married Mr. Calvin P. Walrad two years later and moved from Homer to the more cosmopolitan county seat, the market town of Cortland. Five years passed before their son Alfred (named for his grandfather Chamberlain) was born; then Sarah died in 1871, when little Alfred was only three. Grace doesn't specify the cause of her sister Sarah's untimely death, but it may have been a second childbirth. The tragic losses, and the time and circumstances of this family remind one of Louisa Alcott and her *Little Women*.

Samantha's parents, Rufus and Nancy Boies, were in Homer during the loss of three of the four Chamberlain girls. In their old age they went to live with Samantha's younger brother William, (the one-year-old in the pioneer ox wagon) in Cortland. Nancy was the first to die at age 76 in 1856. She had remained a very religious woman. From her obituary in the Homer newspaper:

> In the last three years of her life, she was a great sufferer. From the effects of a fracture of a limb she never recovered; and a complication of disorders subjected her almost incessantly to excruciating pains. Yet she was very patient. She received all as from God; leaning upon him, as holy and wise, with an unfaltering trust.[54]

Rufus survived Nancy by four years, passing on April 1, 1860, at the age of 83. From his obituary:

---
53   Ibid.
54   Obituary, Cortland Standard, ca. June 29, 1856.

He remained in connection with [the Congregational Church] until his death, attentive to its ordinances and ever ready in his quiet way to bear his share of its burdens and to do his share of the labors incident to the relation. Those who have known him in business affairs speak of his unimpeachable probity. He was one of the founders of the Academy in this place and was ever its ardent friend.... To Capt. Boies is Homer indebted for a considerable share of the reputation which it has long enjoyed as a place of staid moral worth.[55]

The Civil War was raging during the years Samantha and Alfred's youngest girl, Grace, was a student at Cortland Academy. There were no battles in New York State, but many young Homer men, friends and classmates of Grace and her older sisters, joined up and fought for the Union.

The freedom network of the Underground Railway was active in Homer before the War began. Escaped slaves traveled by night up the Tioughnioga River valley from Binghamton to Syracuse, on their way north to freedom in Canada. They knew they could stop at the home of Deacon Oren Cravath for food, rest, and shelter; the deacon's place was a "station" on the Underground Railway. Though Samantha and Alfred attended church with the Cravath family, they were much more conservative, concerned mainly with their family, the farm, and neighbors, rather than the wider national picture. The Deacon finally lost his patience with the stolid people of Homer when he arranged for a speech from the great black abolitionist Frederick Douglass in 1851, at which occasion, the famous orator was pelted with rotten eggs. Disgusted, "Oren Cravath resigned as deacon of the Congregational Church, sold his farm, and moved to Oberlin, Ohio, where there were more people

---

55   Ibid., ca. April 2, 1860.

*The Reading of the Emancipation Proclamation
By Francis Bicknell Carpenter, 1864*

of his way of thinking and a more pronounced movement for the abolition of slavery."[56] It's very unlikely that the Chamberlains were among the egg throwers; they were a well-respected, genteel farming family who preserved their reputation.

Francis Bicknell Carpenter, born in Homer in 1830, was between Samantha and her daughters in age, but no doubt the families were acquainted. As a youth, Frank demonstrated artistic talent, much to his farmer father's dismay. His father considered art foolish nonsense until young Frank's mother showed him a portrait of herself, painted by Frank. "The vulnerable spot in father Carpenter's heart was touched. He himself was the next sitter and then the battle was won."[57]

In 1863, Francis Bicknell Carpenter proposed to President Abraham Lincoln that an historical painting should be done to commemorate the Emancipation Proclamation. His proposal was

---
56   Blodgett, op. cit., p. 253.
57   Ibid., p. 244.

accepted and he spent six months at the White House working on the project, using the state dining room as his studio. President Lincoln joked, "Do you think you could make a good looking man out of me?" The monumental painting went on a national tour after the War, and now hangs in a corridor of the US Capitol.

This is another story of the American Civil War and a distant family connection. Justus Albert Boies never lived in Homer. He was Samantha's 35-years-younger cousin, the youngest son of her father Rufus's youngest brother, a judge who was also named Justus. These Boieses were a highly-educated family in Northampton, MA, whose men were dedicated to the law. It's unlikely that the two cousins ever met. Justus was 21 and studying law with his brother-in-law, Judge Edward Pitkin Cowles, in New York City, when war was declared in April, 1861. He marched with the New York Volunteers to Washington, where he was promoted to Captain, but by his own choice he had his rank reduced to Lieutenant.

Young Justus was serving on the staff of Major-General Frank Blair as the United States fought for Union control of the Mississippi River at Vicksburg, Mississippi on May 22, 1863, when he suffered a cannon shot through the leg. He was evacuated by train accompanied by his lawyer brother-in-law, and brought to the military hospital in Chicago, Illinois. After his shattered leg was amputated, his mother and sisters rushed from Northampton and New York City to his side to care for him. He lingered for three weeks in the hospital, and died on the 28th of June, 1863, at age 22. "He was a youth of bright promise, of fine culture, polished manners and rare attainments," said his obituary in a Chicago newspaper. A Presbyterian funeral was held at the Marine hospital in Chicago, after which his remains were taken under military escort to the train for burial in Northampton.

Chapter 8
Grace Boies Chamberlain

Alfred and Samantha had the same respect for learning as their forbears. Their youngest daughter, our ancestor Grace Boies Chamberlain, started at a Miss Kelsey's school which was run out of the home, then went to the classroom of a Mrs. Day, a missionary returned from India. Grace wrote later that her "girlhood was very happy and I had lots of good times." At twelve, what we would consider middle school age, she went to the Homer Academy where her first teacher was Miss Lucy Gunn. Her father, Alfred, was on the Academy board of trustees. Grace graduated at nineteen from the scientific course at the school, and won three out of the four available prizes offered at commencement. The prizes were given in money, which she used to buy a set of Shakespeare that she kept for the rest of her life.

When Grace was twenty, without higher education, she began to teach in the Primary Department at the Homer Academy, her alma mater. She had been a primary teacher for two and a half years when she decided to further her education at Wells College by the shores of the Finger Lakes in Aurora, NY, another first for our female ancestors. Grace writes, "it was in the early years of the College when Mr. Wells, the founder was alive. He made it very delightful for the girls, extending the hospitality of his beautiful home to the students often and his lovely grounds were always open to us to walk in."[58] Henry Wells had made his fortune as the founder of Wells Fargo.

In the 1870 United States Census, Grace's parents, Alfred and Samantha, are both 64 years old, and they shared their home with their two remaining daughters, Caroline, 34, and Grace, 23. Alfred's real estate was worth $12,500, and his personal property $5,000.

Grace had enjoyed her college years very much, but when she finished, she was needed at home because of family illness. Her sister, Sarah Walrad, three years older, had died in 1871, leaving a little boy, Alfred, who was almost four. Then her 11-years-older unmarried sister Caroline died of tuberculosis the next year, 1872.

Grace was the only sister left out of Samantha and Alfred's four daughters when she became the Preceptress or principal at the Homer Academy, teaching and supervising for five years in the Academy's new building.

Perhaps Grace and her mother Samantha had their little motherless nephew/grandson Alfred at their home often, maybe the little boy even lived with them on the farm, because his widowed father, Calvin P. Walrad, was quite a busy entrepreneur and business leader in nearby Cortland. He had a dry goods and carpet emporium, where he was one of the first merchants to import porcelain goods brought by the clipper ships from China in the 1860's (the family still has some fine examples of this china), and was instrumental in organizing the Cortland Savings Bank in 1866.

Calvin came from German descent, the first in this family who was not Scotch-Irish. His earliest New-World ancestor was Johannes Petrus Walrad, of Canajoharie, in eastern New York, who

---

58   Walrad, op. cit.

was an old man at the time of the 1790 census. In 1837, Johannes's grandson Peter moved his wife and their four young children, of whom Calvin was the youngest at two years old, from Canajoharie to Homer, where Calvin became a student at the Homer Academy.

After being widowed, Calvin P. may have noticed how tender and loving Grace was with his little boy, then he started noticing Grace herself. They were married on September 3, 1878; Grace left the farm to live in Cortland, the county seat, in Calvin P.'s much more opulent home at 13 Lincoln Avenue. At the landing at the top of the white formal stairway at the front of the house, Grace placed a treasure passed down from her mother Samantha and her grandmother Nancy. It was Nancy's spinning wheel, brought from Blandford to Homer in 1812. It was still there in the 1960s.

Grace and Calvin at the time of their wedding

She writes,

> ...in 1880, (June 26) a dear little girl came to live with us, whose name is now Gracie K. Walrad, a very welcome little lady. She was a fat, good-natured girlie, only cried when she had the colic, and has always been a great comfort to us. February 23, 1882, another dear little girl came whose name is Anna Samantha Walrad, a very fat little baby, weighed 8 pounds (Gracie weighed 7) and she grew fatter and fatter until when was 6 months she weighed 20 pounds (Gracie weighed 18). These two little girls take a great deal of comfort together, and their father and mother and big brother take a great deal of comfort with them.[59]

Little Gracie, the not-so-fat older sister, became our ancestor. This was the first generation of the family to leave agricultural pursuits completely behind and successfully embrace business and commerce.

When the two little girls, Gracie and Anna, were babies in 1882 and 1883, and their half-brother Alfred was 14, their grandparents, Samantha and Alfred, now well into their seventies, came into town from the farm to spend the winters. In 1884, they came to stay with the younger family and all three of their grandchildren for the rest of their lives. This was during the administration of President Chester A. Arthur of Vermont.

In 1885, the year before she died, Samantha made a gift for her namesake, three-year-old grand-daughter Anna Samantha—a linen bedsheet, two narrow pieces hand-sewn together up its length, and hand-hemmed all around in tiny stitches. It might have been part of Samantha's own trousseau, woven from flax grown by her mother Nancy, then cut and reassembled as it wore out, or perhaps

---

59   Ibid.

the center seam was necessary because of the narrow width of the loom. In one corner, Samantha has written in black ink:

Anna S. Walrad

Made by her Grandmother

79 years old

Samantha died first, on April 21, 1886, when she was 80, Alfred followed on September 3, 1891 at the age of 84 years and 10 months. Alfred Chamberlain's obituary in the Cortland Standard praised his character:

> As an agriculturalist, Mr. Chamberlain was thorough, studious and practical, making his chosen vocation the duty of both mind and body. As a neighbor and citizen upright, honest in all matters, ever ready to aid, by work or otherwise, the persevering youth; slow to make new friends, but a staunch support to those whom he knew to be worthy, his memory will be long cherished by all who knew him. In politics he was a Democrat of the old school and although not much given to wordy contention, was ever ready to sustain with sound argument his views on every political question.

Alfred's son-in-law Calvin P. Walrad prospered during the 1880s and 1890s. He was a Republican, the president of the incorporated village of Cortland for two years, on the school board, a director of the Elmira, Cortland & Northern railroad, a Rural Cemetery trustee, and on the boards of directors of the Cortland Silk Mill and the Presbyterian Church. He was a real estate entrepreneur, building between thirty and forty houses in Cortland. He was

— THE STORY OF AN AMERICAN FAMILY —

13 Lincoln Avenue circa 1883. Seated: Samantha Boies Chamberlain (the only known picture of her) and Alfred Lyon Chamberlain. Standing: their daughter Grace Chamberlain Walrad.

the embodiment of an American Victorian gentleman—rising from humble origins to local prominence through intelligence, hard work, and a generous nature. When Calvin P. Walrad died of kidney disease at 81 in 1916, the *Cortland Standard* reported, "...this morning Cortland lost one of her most influential and successful citizens, a man prominent, not only in financial and business circles, but in the religious life of the city and in humane work in city, county, and state, and in every good work with which Cortland is connected."

We are fortunate that Calvin and Grace were interested and wealthy enough to take advantage of the new technology of photography. There are many beautiful studio portraits of the family from this point on.

Alfred Chamberlain with Granddaughters

— The Story of An American Family —

Grace Walrad, Gracie and Anna, 1891

Gracie and Anna were very happy growing up in Calvin and Grace's 13-room house on Lincoln Avenue. They were well-loved, and their parents were prosperous enough to provide them with everything they needed. And because their mother, Grace Chamberlain, came from a successful local pioneer family, and their father, though not a native, was a respected local businessman, president of the bank and active in church and community, the girls and their older half-brother, Alfred, enjoyed a prominent social standing in the small city of Cortland.

Gracie learned to read at home before she was six. She and Anna started at Miss Emily Simms' school when they were eight and six years old respectively. By the late 1880's New York's system of coal-powered steam trains was well developed, and Grace and Anna's parents would take them visiting or shopping by train to Syracuse or even New York City. The "cars" went out to the nearby Finger Lakes, where the family enjoyed visiting old friends and picnicking.

As Gracie grew into a lovely teenager, she became ever more social. She and her friends at Cortland Academy formed the "Poultry Club", a loose collection of Presbyterian boys and girls that enjoyed one another's company with skating parties, picnics, or musical evenings. At least one of the boys in this group, Arthur Dunn, fell fast in love with Gracie, but she just didn't have the same feelings for him.

Gracie at 18

She graduated from the Cortland Normal School, which is now the State University of New York at Cortland, thinking she would follow her mother and grandmother into teaching, but that career was finished after one day spent as a substitute in a Cortland elementary school. Gracie was really happiest at home with her beloved parents and sister. Her father's wealth made it easy for her to be a young woman of leisure. Her gifts and talents were domestic; she sewed her own clothes, embroidered and monogrammed all her table linen, helped around the house, enjoyed visiting a wide circle of friends every day and entertaining often. She taught Sunday School at the Presbyterian Church, and wrote and received letters every day.

This was the era of calling cards, the family would sit out on the piazza, or front porch, on warm evenings and receive visitors, people would stop in for dinner.

Gracie had a busy and happy life as a single young woman, immersed in the love and support of her family and the friends she had known since birth. Her life at this time is captured in a random selection from her diary when she was twenty-four:

> July 8, 1904: Went up to Mrs. Magee's this morning and Emily came back with us and we embroidered. Went to drive this afternoon and then down to see Mrs. Alley. Father came home on the late train. Mother went to Tully with Mrs. Wiltsie. Nan and I worked around all morning. Went to Preble with Louie in the automobile tonight.

It's no wonder that she put off marriage for several years.

But, in 1908, Gracie's father Calvin made the acquaintance of Frank Wray McKee, a 30-year-old bachelor engineer on assignment in Cortland from one of the great steel mills of Pittsburgh, Pennsylvania. He was supervising the installation of an electric open-hearth furnace at the Wickwire Brothers' wire manufacturing mill. Calvin was impressed with the young man and invited him to dine with the family at the big round table at 13 Lincoln Avenue. How the spark got started is lost to history, but years later, Gracie still remembered this dinner and told the story to her daughter.

Frank W. McKee was Scotch-Irish. The first McKee, Thomas of County Down, Northern Ireland, had arrived in America through Philadelphia in 1774 at the age of 26, just in time for the American Revolution. He fought in the Battles of Brandywine

Frank W. McKee, c. 1907

and Germantown in Pennsylvania, camped with the troops and General Washington at Valley Forge during the winter of 1777–1778, went on to fight at the Battle of the Cowpens in 1781, and the Battle of Yorktown, where he was privileged to witness the surrender of Lord Cornwallis to General Washington in September of 1781. Back at home, he and his Scotch-Irish wife, Martha Hoge, with their children worked their way west through Pennsylvania farming in a way very similar to that of Gracie's family.

Frank's maternal grandfather, William Bradford Sprague, was a pharmacist who fought in the Civil War when he was over forty. Frank's own father Robert J. McKee, (October 24, 1854–June 30, 1877) had drowned in the Ohio River in 1877 at age 23, leaving three little boys. Frank was the youngest, an infant of four months. As his mother, Nancy Sprague McKee struggled to support the boys, Frank was often fostered by his veteran grandfather, who was originally from Vermont and his grandmother, Sarah Ann McQuaide Sprague.

Robert S., Frank W., and John S. McKee c. 1882

Frank's early years weren't all struggle. At some point he played baseball for the Langeloth Giants. (see the arrow)

Though they came from a similar ethnic and Presbyterian background, this couple had not grown up together, nor had their parents even been acquainted. Education, industrial development, the ease of rail travel, and a vastly improved postal system made it possible for them to get together. Their courtship was chaperoned by Grace's younger sister, Anna. There is a photo of the three of them on what looks like an excursion boat called the *Tuscarora*, with Grace and Anna standing close together several feet away from Frank.

The wedding was held at home in Cortland on Tuesday, June 23, 1908, at eight thirty at night. Frank's mother, Nancy Sprague McKee, attended from Pennsylvania. Grace's family had engraved invitations, announcements, and "at home" cards printed.

— The Story of An American Family —

Grace's best friend Olive Edgecomb wrote to her uncle about the wedding ceremony, explaining that:

...you escaped a very hot time by not being there. They tried not to ask very many but it was hard to draw the lines and so the rooms were pretty well crowded. Then just as the bride was ready to come down the gas all over the house went out and there was a great scurrying around for [oil] lamps at the last minute which of course heated things up more.

...Grace was married in the sitting room so that people could see from the parlor, dining room and porch. I never saw her look better. She wore a most becoming dress of white messaline with some old lace and a long veil....Annie was maid of honor and four of us...held two daisy chains instead of ribbons to make an aisle for the bridal party to walk down. The house was trimmed with daisies and buttercups and pink roses and my how we did work trimming it! Most of the flowers were gotten the day before, but some more daisies had to be picked for the chain at the last minute and it was after five o'clock before we all got through....The bride and groom left about eleven for Homer where they took the N.Y. train but we showered them well with confetti and rice before they left [the house] and again at the station where we all went down to give them a last send-off.

After they had left the house and the crowd had thinned out a little we had a lively Virginia reel while the orchestra was there to play for us. Everybody was feeling fine and we had a very rollicking time. Arthur Dunn [a former admirer of Grace's] seemed to be reconciled to his loss enough to cakewalk through the Virginia reel. He gave Grace a pie knife and someone said it must have been meant for a lemon pie knife....

Was Arthur feeling sour as a lemon pie because Gracie married another man?

Wednesday's *Cortland Standard* provided a few more details of the ceremony.

A pretty June wedding occurred at the home of Mr. and Mrs. Calvin P. Walrad, 13 Lincoln Ave. at 8:30 o'clock last night, when their older daughter, Miss Grace Katherine Walrad, was united in marriage to Frank Wray McKee of Beaver, Pa.

The ceremony was performed in the presence of about one hundred guests by Rev. David S. Curry, pastor of the First Presbyterian Church. The bride was attired in a gown of white messaline trimmed with duchesse lace. She wore a veil and carried a shower bouquet of lilies of the valley. She was attended by her sister, Miss Anna Walrad, as maid of honor, who wore blue messaline and carried white sweet peas. James Conrad of Pittsburg, Pa., acted as best man. The bridal party passed through an aisle formed of daisy chains held by friends of the bride.

The house was attractively decorated with ferns, and daisies, the decorations being in charge of Miss Clara Hastings of Homer.

Mr. and Mrs. McKee left on the 11:48 train for Montreal, Quebec and other Canadian points. They will be at home

— The Story of An American Family —

Gracie in her wedding gown

after July 20 at Beaver, Pa., where the groom has an excellent position with the Jones & Loughlin Steel Co. The bride is a graduate of the Normal and one of Cortland's most popular and attractive young ladies.

The bride was the recipient of a large number of gifts, including a large quantity of silver, some beautiful brass, cut glass, china etc.

Her hair was in a "Gibson Girl" updo, lace veil cascading to the floor. Her dress was white, high-necked to the chin, wasp-waisted, and floor length, silk with satin touches, leg o'mutton sleeves and elbow-length white gloves.

During their wedding trip to Canada and Niagara Falls, Gracie turned 28. The couple then settled into married life in Beaver, Pennsylvania, close to the steel business in Pittsburgh where 31-year-old Frank was an electrical engineer. It must have been a challenging adjustment for Gracie to leave her family and her comfortable social life in Cortland, and start over again in a new place. She was inexperienced with loneliness.

Two years passed before Grace and Frank's first baby came, on September 26, 1910, a girl named Anna after Grace's sister. Grace's mother, Grace Chamberlain Walrad, came on the train from Cortland to help. Tragically, baby Anna only lived 13 days, and passed away on October 8. On October 10, Frank's friend and best man, James Conrad, wrote to him,

> Mother has just written me of the very sad news of the baby's birth and sudden death. I am so sorry to hear of this, but I am glad to hear that Grace is getting along nicely and is holding up so well. The mother has so much to withstand and in her case particularly so. But Mother thinks Grace is getting

along well. The Lord's ways seem pretty hard some times and almost more than can be borne. Give my very best love and deepest sympathy to Grace in her trouble. Jim.

It's odd (to me) that Jim extended sympathy to Grace only; Frank had lost his baby too. One hopes that Grace's mother, who was so well acquainted with untimely death after losing three sisters, was a great comfort to heartbroken couple.

They had to wait three years for another baby, though Gracie was getting into her thirties. Robert Bradford McKee was born in March, 1913, a sturdy, serious boy who, as the oldest, had many professional photos done. He was named for his paternal grandfather who drowned in the Ohio River, and he was always called Bobby by his family. Bobby was an excellent student, went to Rensselaer Polytechnic Institute in Troy, NY, and became a successful civil engineer for the Army Corps of Engineers, a train-spotting hobbyist, and a world-traveler who was very devoted to Gracie. He never married and lived in New York State all his life.

Robert Bradford McKee on the porch with his grandfather, Calvin P. Walrad.

Two years later, in February, 1915, came Frank Wray McKee, named for his father. He was known in the family as Buzz, Bobby's first pronunciation of "brother". He became a medical doctor. He was in a Navy hospital boat at D-Day, June 6, 1944, in the English Channel treating the wounded soldiers evacuated from the beaches of Normandy. After the bombs dropped on Japan in 1945, he treated the liberated Allied POW's in another Navy hospital ship docked in Tokyo. In his later years he worked in medical school administration, living in many different parts of the country. Buzz was married. He and his wife Mary adopted twins, a boy and a girl, in 1957.

Frank, Buzz, Grace and Bobby. Note Frank's camera. c. 1916

In November 1917, a third boy was born, Calvin Walrad McKee, named for Grace's father who had died the year before. Cal was not much like his businessman grandfather. He grew up to be the clown of the family, a very funny man who was married to Harriette and had one daughter. He was an electrical engineer, worked for General Electric and Sylvania, and lived in the suburbs of Philadelphia all of his adult life.

During the World War I years, while these three boys were coming along, the annual steel production of Pittsburgh exceeded the combined output of the nations of Germany and Austria,[60] so the boys' electrical engineer father Frank McKee must have been busy and prosperous.

At last, on March 16, 1919, Gracie, who was now 39, went to the hospital in Beaver and had a little girl, our ancestor Jean Chamberlain McKee. Grace's younger sister Anna wrote from Cortland:

Dear Grace,

This week must be a real vacation with one child instead of three. It is nice to have a girl in the family, and we are anxiously looking forward to seeing her. We don't even know whether her hair is red or not.

I had a brief trip down to New York last week. Mother and Miss Howe seemed to get along very well here. I enjoyed the day at the Hendricks especially. Also the theater Friday night. The meeting made us feel as tho we must go to work again and that wasn't good news.

---

60 Wikipedia.

Arthur Dunn and Ed. Stilson are in New York having been sent down as Y.M.C.A. representatives to bring the boys of the 27th Division home. It is a fine chance to be in the middle of things in camp—if only for a few days. Alfred [Anna and Grace's older half-brother] has had the "flu" so can't march in the parade. The parade is to be the greatest event we have had in these parts.

The weather is so warm that I am considering awnings for the porch. It is about time to move out.

Do stay in the hospital long enough to feel quite strong before going home to your strenuous family. Hoping that all may go well, I am

As ever, Ann.

Jean, Cal, Buzz, Bobby, 1921

Shortly after Jean was born, the now-large family moved to a bigger house at 252 Taylor Avenue in Beaver, PA, and lived there busily and happily until the summer of 1923, when father Frank befriended a stray dog and decided to keep it for the family. During the last week of June, he was trying to cut its nails when the dog bit him. One of Jean's few precious memories of him was witnessing this dog bite at four years old; her father flinched and shouted, "He's got me!"

Dr. McCauley came to treat the wounds, which seemed to heal nicely. The dog was destroyed and its head sent to a lab in Philadelphia to be tested for rabies, but the package went disastrously astray in the mail. By the time it arrived at the lab, the contents were so decomposed that it could not be analyzed. Frank's doctor in Beaver had not believed the dog was rabid, so no Pasteur treatment was offered. Frank became sick about seven weeks after the dog bite.

On August 18, 1923, the *Daily Times* of Beaver ran the front page headline, "RABIES CAUSES DEMISE of WELL KNOWN BEAVER MAN". The article explains, "Four days ago he complained of chills. A nervous condition followed, and then he became affected with what seemed to be a bad cold. Drs. M. M. Mackall of Beaver and John McCauley of Rochester attended him. Dryness and tightening of his throat bothered him according to Dr. Mackall. Yesterday, Mr. McKee became suddenly worse..." When it became clear how dire the situation was, a friend and neighbor, Mr. Foster, "telephoned to Pittsburgh for a specialist in Pasteur treatment. He agreed to come, but upon learning the condition then of the patient, said there was no hope."[61] Frank McKee had one convulsion, and died. At forty-six, he left Grace a widow with four young children.

---

61   Beaver (PA) *Daily Times*, August 18, 1923.

Funeral services were held at the McKee's home in Beaver at 7:30 the night of August 18, conducted by the Rev. A. J. Alexander of the Beaver First Presbyterian Church. The body was taken by train to Cortland later that night for burial. It's quite certain that Grace, Cal (five) and Jean (four) accompanied the body on that train to Cortland. Bobby and Buzz had been there already for a few weeks visiting their grandmother and Aunt Anna. Grace had put the two of them on a train from Beaver to Cortland by themselves with ten-year-old Bobby in charge of eight-year-old-Buzz. Bobby was a very responsible boy. When the rest of the Pennsylvania family arrived in Cortland, the first duty was bury Frank and receive condolences from the many friends Grace still had there. Then Grace, her mother Grace Chamberlain Walrad, and her sister Anna Walrad had some difficult and serious decisions to make.

Calvin P. Walrad, the wealthy Cortland businessman, had left his widow and his unmarried daughter Anna the big house on Lincoln Avenue and a generous investment income when he died in 1916. The half-brother Alfred Walrad was 55 years old by 1923, and had his own family in another town. The three women made the decision that Gracie and the four children should move back to Cortland from Pennsylvania, all to live together at 13 Lincoln Avenue. It must have been quite a change for the elderly grandmother and spinster aunt to welcome such a rambunctious brood into their quiet and sedate home.

It was during this same month of August, 1923, that President Warren G. Harding collapsed and died suddenly of a heart attack in San Francisco following an exhausting tour of the United States and Alaska. Vice President Calvin Coolidge was sworn into office by his own father, a notary public, in Plymouth, Vermont, in the early hours of August 3. This national tragedy involving sudden death could only have added to the McKees' misery.

By the time the Beaver house was sold and the furniture and other belongings packed and sent to Cortland, it was late October or early November 1923, and the children needed to be registered for school in Cortland. Jean was still only four, but Grace got her into kindergarten at the Schermerhorn School anyway. Mr. Smith, the Superintendent of Schools, lived next door, the families had been friends for years, and Grace had no problem asking for a good word from him.

Little Jean had to repeat kindergarten the next year, of course, but it did her no harm. She and her three older brothers did well in school, though she missed having a father. Classrooms then sang patriotic songs (and recited Lord's Prayer and saluted the flag) every day as part of "morning exercises". She remembered singing the line in "My Country 'Tis of Thee", "land where our fathers died", and thinking she was the only one in the class whose father actually had died.

Aunt Anna Walrad became an important figure, almost a second mother, for the children. Before the McKee clan descended, she had taught high school English in Plainfield, NY, founded the Cortland branch of the Red Cross during World War I and served as its Secretary, was a long-time member and Treasurer of the Hospital Board, was very active in the Presbyterian Church, taught Sunday School, and in later years joined the Cortland Historical Society. She had gone to Wellesley College, Class of 1903, near Boston; and as soon as Jean appeared in Cortland, Anna sent a $25 deposit to Wellesley to hold a place for her.

Anna soon determined that the now-large family would not be able to thrive on the same income that she and her elderly mother had enjoyed. So, at age 41, she went to their next door neighbor, Ferdinand E. Smith, the Superintendent of Schools, and proposed that she should open and staff a library at Cortland High School. He was persuaded, but first she would need to get a Master's Degree in Library Science, which was quickly accomplished at Syracuse University. The library was up and running by 1925. Anna continued as Cortland High School librarian for the next twenty-five years, and put all four of her sister Grace's children through college even during the Great Depression.

Anna Samantha Walrad at her Wellesley graduation, 1903

It turned out Anna actually adored going to work in the high school every day. She guided the teens through all their research, went to all the football and basketball games, and kept a chart of where each of her Cortland graduates was stationed during World War II. She retired from the library in June of 1950 at age 68. On the day before her death just six months later in January, 1951, she reminisced with a friend about how much she missed the students, helped out at the blood bank, then in the evening, cheered the Cortland Purple Tigers on to a basketball victory. She went home to sleep in the house where she was born, and never woke up.[62]

Back in the 1920s and 1930s, Jean McKee was enjoying a happy childhood on Lincoln Avenue. The two older boys, Bobby and Buzz, had a very close bond which effectively excluded the third boy, Cal; so Cal took little Jean under his wing with sometimes amusing or alarming results. There was an old carriage house in the back which had held horses and wagons in Calvin P. Walrad's day. Hay was winched up and stored in the loft with a chute ready to supply it to the horses in their stalls below. By the time this generation moved in, the carriage house had become a garage for the family's Essex automobile. Cal convinced Jean that the chute, which was completely vertical, would make a fun slide. She did it once, apparently without suffering serious or permanent injury.

Cal heard the women of the house worrying about money and came up with a brilliant solution. He gave Jean, who might have been five, one of their mother's tin measuring cups, then walked her the two blocks down to Main Street. He told her not to cry, but just to look very sad, sit on the step of the five and dime store, and hold out the cup to passersby. Cal melted away around the corner. Fortunately for all concerned, the first passerby was their mother Grace, who scooped up little Jean and took her home.

---

62 *The Purple Pennant*, Cortland High School newspaper, January 18, 1951.

— Susan Billings —

Jean and Cal

Real money problems came a few years later when the stock market crashed in October, 1929. Grandfather Walrad's careful and judicious investments were suddenly worthless. The big house on Lincoln Avenue belonged to the family outright, but money was tight. The flush days of Calvin P. Walrad were over. The family scrimped and saved what they could with four growing children to feed, the boiler down in the cellar wanting coal, and Calvin's big house, which was now sixty-five years old. The Scotch-Irish genius for thrift and making-do had not gone away.

Grace Boies Chamberlain Walrad, Calvin's widow and the children's grandmother, died January 11, 1927, at the age of 79. In her long life she had known her own grandparents, Rufus and Nancy Boies, the pioneers who had been born to the American

Grace Boies Chamberlain Walrad

Revolution. She herself had been born during the Mexican War, lived through the Civil War, Spanish-American War, and World War I. She had lived with ox carts, horse buggies, steam trains, automobiles, and airplanes. From her birth in 1847 to her 1927 death, she lived under an astounding 20 US presidents (counting Grover Cleveland twice for his 2 non-sequential terms), from James K. Polk to Calvin Coolidge. She voted Republican in the few elections held since women got the vote (1920), and was a life-long and faithful Presbyterian. Jean remembered her as a loving grandmother who liked to read stories, and the sweetness of her scent when they sat close together.

The thirties brought Cortland High School graduation to the McKee children. Bobby was valedictorian of the Cortland High School class of 1931, and Buzz followed as the second family valedictorian in 1933. Cal, class of 1935, and Jean in 1937, were more middling students, though Jean was on the honor roll, but they certainly had a lot of fun.

— CHAPTER 9 —
Out of Cortland

The three boys had successful college careers, all within New York State, and went on to fulfilling professional lives. Jean started out at Bucknell College in Lewisburg, Pennsylvania, but, finding Lewisburg rather limiting, transferred after two years to Simmons College in Boston. She blossomed in Boston, made wonderful female friends that she kept for life, and honed her husband-hunting skills far from the small town of Cortland. She worked hard at Simmons with a major in Publication, was active in extracurricular activities including singing, and had plenty of dates with young men from Harvard and MIT.

Jean graduated from Simmons in May, 1941, spent the summer at home in Cortland working at Woolworth's and anxiously applying by mail for jobs in publication in Boston. The two years at Simmons had convinced her that the big city was the place to be. She aced an interview in Boston, and was offered a clerical position at *Skating*, the magazine of the Boston Skating Club. Here's a quote from her diary of August 16, 1941, "Today, Girl, today—I

Jean's Simmons graduation picture

officially became a career woman. I got the job! Lord, it's wonderful! I don't believe that I actually got it!...It was at 4:30 I found out. Mrs. Blanchard sent a special [delivery letter] to tell me." Next day: "I woke up thinking 'Something different' and then I remembered. A Job, Girl! Oh, I hope I make good down there!"

Lots of clothes shopping, movie going, shorthand practicing and friend visiting followed. On August 27, "Time draws near, Girl. It's different this time. Talk of apartments + buying food + going to work every day—it's not the same at all. I'm thrilled more than frightened. Hope I stay that way. Finished my hat today. It's a little limp but it doesn't look like a sleeve anymore." Her brother Bob, who was attending Harvard Business School, and Annie Grant, her best friend from Simmons, drove up to Cortland from Boston. They took Jean and her trunks full of career girl clothes back to Boston on Labor Day. She checked into her rooming house and started work the next day.

— Susan Billings —

> My panic had all left me by the time I arrived this morning + I sailed into my career with flags flying. They mistook me mostly for an addressograph, but I did take dictation from Mrs. Blanchard + had no trouble at all, that is unless I get the letters back tomorrow to be redone. Time went fast. Grant [Annie] called me. Stan [her sort-of boyfriend] came about 6:15 + we went to a horrible Indian place to eat + me spoiling for steak + French fries. Danced out into the Totem Pole.

She had dates almost every night, and had a big crush on Win, a handsome co-worker at the magazine, all while Stanley and Stanley's mother believed she was going to marry him. October 30, Win asked her out, but she had already made a date to go to "a stinking B-school [Harvard Business School] dance with a sawed off bit of anemic manhood. Maybe it's best—I don't know. I have a theory in the back of my mind that for the beautiful peace of the office I shouldn't go out with him [Win], But he is darling."

My theory is that the "sawed off bit of anemic manhood" was my father. Howard and Jean met on a blind date in October of 1941, an unheard-of arrangement in previous generations. He was impressed, but, as you can see from her diary entries, she wasn't. By the time they met, he had his MBA (though he still was active socially at the Business school) and was employed as a chemical engineer at a new Cambridge research and development firm called Arthur D. Little, located in an office building on Memorial Drive.

The next day she writes, "Howard Hamacker [sic] called me up this morning....Stanley called and I refused dates for tonite + Sunday. Date came at 8:30. [Howard]...Beloved B-school. Nothing has changed. Still liquor—still beautiful women." Two days later, "Howard and I played bridge, [with another couple] all afternoon. Gosh, it seemed good to play. Then we toasted hotdogs in the fireplace + drank quantities of beer....Despite the fact that Howard comes to my shoulder + looks like Piglet, I like him!" On November 27, "Howard Hamacker [sic] called + asked me to a cocktail party Saturday. Ernest called Win + asked him to bring me out to Lexington (!) either tonite or tomorrow. Win wouldn't go tonite + I couldn't tomorrow but I imagine it's just as well. Win asked me for a date a week from Saturday. Ahead of time, by gosh! Best of all, Al-baby wrote + asked for a date next Friday night. Cheers!"

Jean often said she would have starved on her $20 a week paycheck from *Skating* if it weren't for having a dinner date almost every night. "I called Bob [her brother] up + he came + fetched me + we put away a tidy meal. Came back + got dressed. Stanley came about 9:00. We proceeded to the Beachcomber [a nightclub]. I've been there with Fred Bruce, Wholesome Colson + now Stanley, and for each my affection has been at a minimum."

The next day "Howard appeared about 5:30 + we went to Shay Smith's + drank quarts of Old Fashioneds. We started making love because we were drunk, but after a small steak + coffee we felt the same way. I don't know whether it was just an incident with no past or future or not, but it was lovely." Next day, "Just got in the house when Howard called. I'd like to state chronologically what happened from then on. We went to the Circle Grill for a couple of beers. We went to the B school + Howard dictated an article + I typed it. We went to the Butterfly Coffee Shop for waffles. We went to Ort's for beer. We went to some joint on Brookline for beer. Came home. Gosh, I like him!"

December 1:
I've been trying to analyze feelings again, Girl. Falling in love is, for the moment, out of the question. I like too many men too much to concentrate on one. But there's something about Howard that appeals to a little higher level in

me than I usually have my affections on. He's one of the few of this season's crop with whom one has any feeling that a lifetime would be desirable. All of which I merely mention in passing. I'm probably much too cold-blooded about life.

December 8, the day after President's Roosevelt's "Day of Infamy", when Japanese bombers attacked Pearl Harbor, Hawaii:

We went to war today, Girl, and suddenly for the first time in years my little feeble fickle loves and my date average seem awfully unimportant + more than a little silly. I wish I could have lived in peace. But no normal life span is peaceful—nor has been—nor, human nature being human, will be. I feel helpless and parasitical and morbid.

The next day she is back to normal.

Girl, I don't suppose I'll ever have as many men in my life again as I have now. How the dickens do women stay true to one for a lifetime? Win asked me out for Friday night. I said yes. Howard called and asked me for tonite + I was awfully sorry I couldn't. When I got home I had letters from Stan + Al-baby. Al didn't say anything but it was comforting to hear from him.

December 20:
Howard called this morning + asked me to go country dancing. [Brother] Bob and I [Christmas] shopped all afternoon + when I got back Dickerman called + promised to get me back for Howard if I'd go out to dinner. Ate with him + Jack Gould + Kip Young. Fun. The dancing was a howl. Howard + I consistently went the wrong way until we were

ostracized. Came back to George Lenart's apt. Gosh I like Howard.

Jean went to the Ice Capades with Win, the officemate, on New Year's Eve, and summed up her 1941 at the end of the diary:

> This is the end of something out of a play—this year has been the maddest, gayest, happiest time a girl could know. There couldn't be another like it—and I've no idea what to expect this next time. I only know that I am grateful for this brilliant erratic gem of 1941 where anything was possible and all of it happened. There's been so much laughter + so little anguish—I fear a balance due me that is inevitable. But come what may, there was one year that stands for glamour, for heady excitement + for everything modern + smooth. Believe me, I am grateful.

As the United States' participation in World War II accelerated, many of Jean's current and potential boyfriends signed up or were drafted for service and shipped overseas. Howard was the exception. Because of his remarkably poor eyesight, he was rated 4-F, but contributed to the war effort by employing his Harvard Business School education in Washington DC, working for the Office of Price Administration supervised by the economist John Kenneth Galbraith. The Office was concerned with price stabilization, consumer protection, and the rationing of goods made scarce by the war—gasoline and heating oil, automobiles, coffee, sugar, processed foods, meat, and materials like nylon and rubber. Arthur D. Little did its own bit for the war by giving many of its younger employees a leave of absence, with their jobs guaranteed when they came back.

Thanks to excellent train service in the country during wartime, Howard made frequent trips from the nation's capital back to Boston to pursue his courtship of Jean during the winter and spring of 1942. He loved her wit, her spirit, and her long, glossy auburn hair, and she thought he was the most intelligent man she had ever met. At some point, the couple took a drive up to Hampton Beach on the short New Hampshire coast. Howard proposed: "Can you think of any reason why we shouldn't get married?" Jean's short answer to his awkward proposal; "NO!"

Unfortunately, there are no photographs of the wedding, perhaps because the photographers had gone off to war. It took place at 13 Lincoln Avenue in Cortland, just as Jean's mother Grace's wedding had, on the evening of October 17, 1942, 165 years to the day after the birth of Jean's ancestor Rufus Boies, though they weren't aware of the interesting coincidence. The brothers all were there, including Buzz, who had recently signed on to the US Navy. His new wife, Mary Mulligan McKee, greeted her sister-in-law Jean for the first time by drawling, "Oh good, now we won't have to stop in Boston" (before Buzz was shipped off to the European theater from New York). Bobby walked Jean down the front stairs past Nancy Gibbs Boies' spinning wheel. One story has survived: just as the Presbyterian minister was reading the ceremonial words, "If any man present knows of any reason why these two should not be joined together in marriage, speak now or...forever hold your peace," there was a loud and frantic knocking at the side porch. Jean's brother Cal rushed to open the door. It was the ice cream man delivering dessert for the reception!

They took their honeymoon in Western Massachusetts, traveling by train because gasoline for the car was so difficult to come by during the war. They visited the Jacob's Pillow Dance Company and Tanglewood, the site of the Boston Symphony Orchestra's summer home. Jean was getting a taste of Howard's passion for high culture, yet it was unknown to her that they were traveling in the wagon wheel tracks of her great-grandmother's pioneering trek with the family 130 years earlier in 1812.

Howard Hamacher

Wm. Hamacher & Martha Jane McTarsney

Our ancestor Howard Hamacher was born in Marshalltown, Iowa, September 18, 1915. His parents, Howard Hamacher Sr. and Ethel Louise Hutchison were married on September 23, 1914, in Guthrie Center, Iowa, by the Rev. John Carl Orth.

Howard Hamacher Sr.'s father was William Harrison Hamacher, born in Indiana in 1842. He was a private in the Civil War. His mother was Martha Jane McTarsney whose parents had immigrated to Indiana from County Tyrone, Ireland, to escape the Great Potato Famine.

The very first Hamacher in America was Johannes Adamus Hamacher, known as Adam, a Mennonite born in 1718 in the Rhine Valley of Germany. He sailed from Rotterdam in 1740 on the ship *Samuel and Elizabeth* with his new wife, Eva Maria Licht and a large community of Mennonites, landed in Philadelphia and spent the rest of his life farming and working in Lancaster County,

PA. Their son, our ancestor David Hamacher, served with several of his brothers in the American Revolution.

Howard Sr. had a laundry business in Marshalltown, and Ethel was a schoolteacher. Sometime in 1918 the dumbwaiter which carried the finished laundry up to the street-level store-front broke down. Howard Sr. was in the basement trying to repair it when the platform fell, injuring him fatally. Ethel and two-year-old Howard were left on their own. They lived in Des Moines with Ethel's mother, Mrs. Hutchison, for a while, I know this because Howard told me that he accidently shot his grandmother in the foot with a B–B gun when he was five. She was not seriously injured.

Howard & Ethel at home, 1527 6th Ave., Des Moines, Iowa.

Howard's high school yearbook picture

Later, after Grandmother's death, they moved west to the Spokane, Washington area, to live near a brother of Howard Sr.'s. Ethel became a teacher at Northwest Business College.

When Howard was 13, Ethel had some kind of abdominal surgery, perhaps a hysterectomy. She became infected with peritonitis, and died. Howard was orphaned. Losing his mother was devastating. He was affected by this loss for the rest of his life. He was never able to attend another funeral after hers, and was repressed to the point of being almost unable to express the simplest of emotions. The nicest thing he ever said to me was that I reminded him of his mother.

He went to live with his father's brother, Elwin (known as Ed) Hamacher, and his wife Mabel in Spokane, Washington state. Ed was a WWI veteran and the Vice President of Spokane's Duffy-Hamacher Lumber Company. The childless couple had adopted a baby son named John who was about five years old when Howard came to stay with the family. Howard attended Lewis & Clark High School where he managed the football team and made excellent grades, especially in math and science.

After graduation in 1933, he drove with three friends south through the mountains and desert to the California Institute of Technology in Pasadena, where he majored in chemical engineering. They were mentioned in the *Bakersfield Californian* paper when they crashed the car on Howard's 18th birthday, September 18, and all went to the local hospital with cuts and bruises.

One of his jobs at Cal Tech was parking cars for the Rose Bowl, and he spent at least one summer with the Civilian Conservation Corps (CCC), a Roosevelt New Deal program, chopping brush in the Rocky Mountains for fire prevention, and uprooting gooseberry bushes to interrupt the reproductive cycle of Rocky Mountain spotted fever ticks. The young men of the CCC lived in camps run by the Army, where they were clothed, fed, and paid $30 a month, which they were expected to send home.

In 1937, after graduation from Cal Tech, he was employed for a year at the Selby foundry in Crockett, CA, where some of the work consisted of shoveling scrap metal into a giant furnace. He applied his chemical engineering degree in refining the melted metal into alloys or pure ingots. He once mentioned a shipful of Chinese copper coins with square holes in the middle which motored up the Carquinez Strait to be dumped and melted down at the foundry. Whenever gold was being processed, the men had to have two sets of clothes; they weren't allowed to leave the foundry with the clothes they worked in. The Selby location was so polluted, it became a Superfund site in the 1980s, and is now paved over.

Howard had taken this job, sleeping and eating at a boarding house in the tiny town of Crockett, in order to save enough money to get his MBA at Harvard Business School. He drove across the country in the late summer of 1938, arriving in Rhode Island on September 22 or 23, to stay a few days with the family of a college friend. He had driven right into the immediate aftermath of the Great New England Hurricane of 1938. With difficulty, he finally arrived at Harvard to begin his two-year program.

At twenty-three, Howard had never been east of the Mississippi, and he fell completely in love with Boston. The eastern college women and career girls were fabulous, liquor flowed freely, and he enjoyed the challenge and stimulation of the Business School. One of his classmates was Robert McNamara, future president of Ford Motor Company and Lyndon Johnson's Secretary of Defense during the Vietnam War. Howard made some life-long friends who had recently arrived as refugees from the gathering storm in Europe. The sophisticated sparkle of the city was a completely new experience.

After their wedding and honeymoon, Jean and Howard moved into an apartment in a nice building near Harvard Square in Cambridge, and they both continued working; she at *Skating* magazine, and he at Arthur D. Little.

Early in 1944, Jean began her first pregnancy, and the couple followed the popular trend of moving to the suburbs to raise the family. They bought their first home, a three-bedroom, one-bath, at 9 Richard Road in Lexington for $7500. They adopted a pair of dachshunds, Seidel and Gretel, who soon had a litter of their own. Howard continued to commute to Arthur D. Little by train, walking down the hill to the stop, while Jean stayed home, kept house, waited for the baby, and made some good friends among the ladies in the neighborhood. Howard must have been thrilled to be starting his own family (though he would never have let on), as his parents' early deaths had made his own childhood so sad and lonely.

Labor began on the morning of October 23, Howard dropped Jean off (!) at Symmes Arlington Hospital. When she asked about getting into a room, the nurse snapped at her, "Don't you know there's a war on!" as if the corridors were lined with injured soldiers (they weren't). It was customary to sedate laboring mothers heavily, and when Jean woke up, she had to ask about the gender of the baby. Susan Chamberlain Hamacher had arrived at 10 PM, a six and a half pound girl with all her fingers and toes and a dimple in the chin like her father. Mothers then were kept in the hospital for two weeks, allowed to dangle their feet over the edge of the bed after ten days. When Jean and Susan came home, 64-year-old Grace McKee soon arrived from Cortland to help with her first grandchild.

On April 12, 1945, Jean was bottle feeding six-month-old Susan and listening to the radio when the announcement came through that President Franklin D. Roosevelt had died of a cerebral hemorrhage in Warm Springs, Georgia. Jean was so shocked and dismayed at the news that she absent mindedly popped the bottle from the baby's lips. Howls ensued, and mother was quickly forced to recover and tend to the screaming reality in her lap. The long and devastating war which had taken so many of their friends and associates was still going strong, and Jean said later that she couldn't imagine how the United States could go on without FDR.

Susan was a great hit in the family, and, as is typical of the first child, lots of photos were taken.

*New grandmother &
new mother 1944*

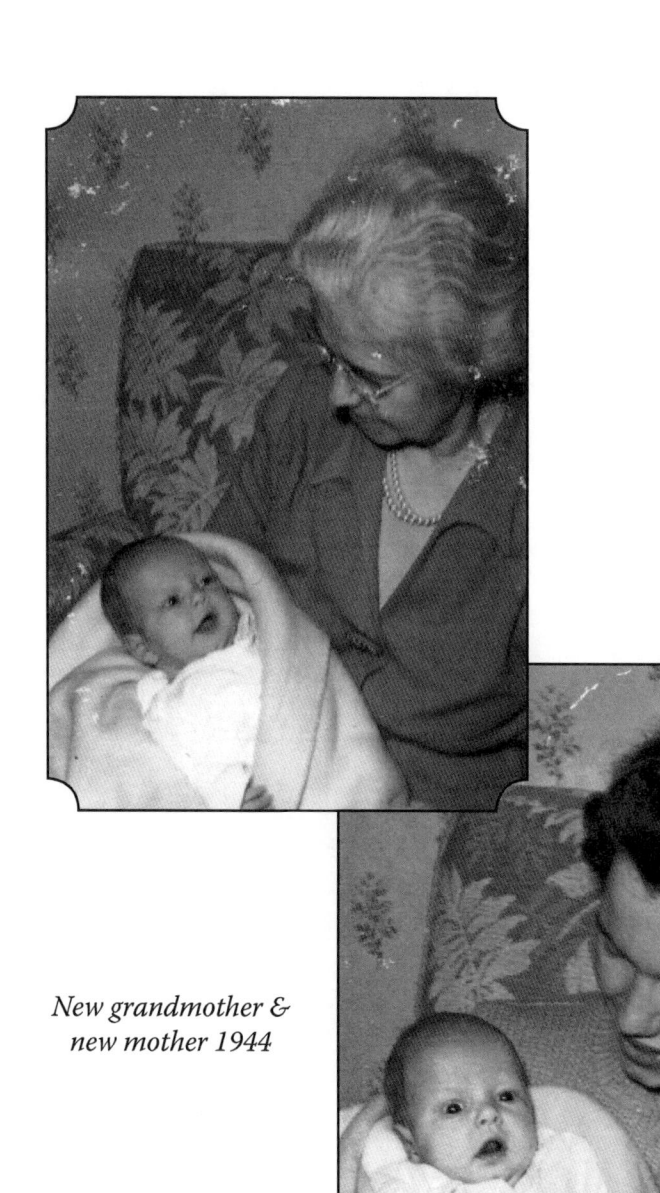

— The Story of An American Family —

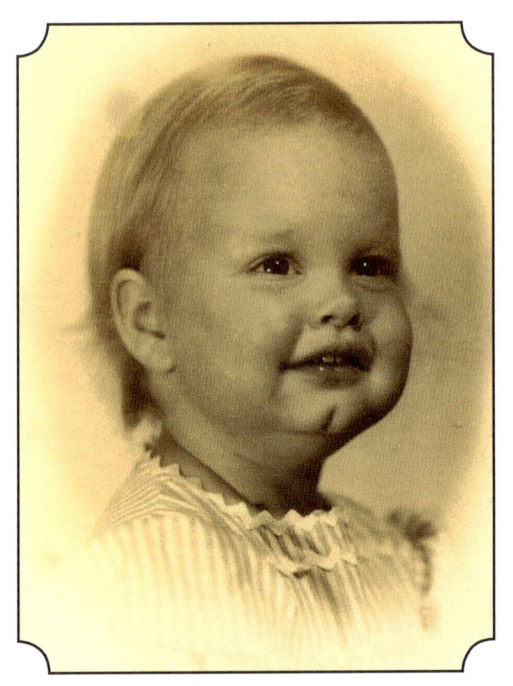

Susan at one

Howard & Jean with Susan at 9 Richard. Dog looking like biting Howard's nose off.

Chapter 10
The Post~War Years & Cultural Change

In the two years after Susan's birth, Jean had two miscarriages. It must have been scary and disappointing to lose those babies, especially as the post-war baby boom had begun and many friends were pregnant. But Jean's mother Gracie encouraged her, "Well, at least you won't mind the time you spend trying!"

John Calvin Hamacher arrived on the Fourth of July, 1948, at the Boston Lying In. For much of his early childhood, John believed that the parades, flags, and fireworks were all in celebration of his birthday.

When John was just 14 months old, Christine McKee Hamacher appeared on September 6, 1949. She pleased Jean especially because, after two blondies like Howard, the Hamachers had a red head! Her hair stayed a lovely strawberry blond for the rest of her

Susan with Christine, 1949

life, while Jean had started to go gray in her thirties, and colored her red hair for the next fifty years.

At Christine's birth, the family moved to the other side of Follen Hill in Lexington, to number 104, where they stayed until the early 1970s. One-O-Four was a new house, built in the years just after the end of the war. It was modern, low and sleek, set among pine trees away from the road. They paid $25,000. In 1950 and 51, the Hamachers built a large addition, with a second garage topped by two bedrooms and a spacious "playroom".

Children didn't slow Howard and Jean's social life. Along with their college friends, Arthur D. Little was a great source of smart and fashionable companions. Dinner and cocktail parties happened every weekend, and babysitters often put the children to bed. The couple reflected post-war America's new world status; young, educated, good-looking, and wealthier than ever before. Neither Jean nor Howard gave a second thought to staying in the places of their birth. Americans were free of those traditional ties and ready to go wherever they found happiness and fulfillment.

These were years of cultural change. The Hamacher children were loosely supervised and wild in ways their ancestors never would have considered. Susan and her friends rocked to Bill Haley and the Comets, did the twist with Chubby Checker, and had mad crushes on both Pat Boone and Elvis Presley, the contrasting faces of adolescent sexuality. Young people would happily get into the parents' alcohol and cigarettes, and the family cars at drive-in movies were pits of passion.

Sometime in the early sixties, Jean became employed at Radcliffe College as an administrative assistant at the Radcliffe Seminars for Independent Studies. It was a fellowship program for women who were outstanding in different fields, mostly art and literature. She became acquainted with some remarkable women from the United States and all over the world: poets, memoirists, abstract painters, a social scientist from India, a Japanese radio personality. She edited books, counseled the high-strung artists, and was a good friend to those who were far from home. She loved the job, and was sad to have to leave it in 1972 when Howard retired from Arthur D. Little.

Howard had been with this very successful firm from near its beginning in about 1940, through its move from rented space on Memorial Drive to a dedicated campus on Route 2 in Cambridge. He served in many different capacities from research and development to administration. He capped his Arthur D. Little career as Treasurer of the company.

The Hamachers traveled extensively all over the world. While the children were still at home there were domestic vacations to Cape Cod, skiing in New Hampshire, camping at Yellowstone National Park, a visit to Salt Lake City. They traveled through California from south (including Tijuana) to north, Oregon, the Smoky Mountains, the Deep South. They took parents-only vacations in Europe. In 1972-1973, when both the girls were married and John was out of the house, they retired to an American development called "Playas de Nosara" on the Pacific in Costa Rica for almost 8 years, where they enjoyed the tropical lifestyle until Howard was diagnosed with early lung cancer and they needed to take advantage of Medicare. He had a lobe removed and actually recovered. In 1980 they sold the house in Costa Rica and built a canal-side home in Englewood, Florida.

It was during the 70s and 80s that they really explored the world visiting Russia, China, Outer Mongolia, Scandinavia, Peru, Chile (even boating into Antarctic waters), Argentina, Uruguay, Bolivia, Brazil, South Africa, Easter Island, Tahiti, Australia, New Zealand, an Alaska cruise, Turkey and Greece, and other countries and regions. Jean sometimes said that Howard enjoyed planning these trips as much as actually going.

The 1960s meant changes for the Hamachers, as they did for almost every family in the United States. Susan graduated from Lexington High School in 1962 with an excellent education and an inquiring mind. In the mistaken belief that it would please her mother, she enrolled at Simmons College in Boston in the Publication course. Freshman year brought the Cuban Missile Crisis on her 18th birthday, and the fear that nuclear holocaust would end her world before it ever got started. In the fall of 1963, President Kennedy was assassinated. Susan rode the MTA home on Friday evening, November 22, where everyone on the train was crying. Thanksgiving that year was a somber affair.

In hindsight, the Kennedy assassination seemed really to kick off much of the cultural change of the sixties. Youth felt victimized. Though she hadn't reached voting age at his election, Susan felt an ownership of and a commitment to Kennedy's presidency. Like many young people, she heard him talking to her, and his handsome looks and dashing demeanor didn't hurt the sense of connection. The new president, Lyndon Johnson of Texas, carried on the

Kennedy policy in Vietnam, a proxy cold-war conflict, and college students all over the country reacted with teach-ins, demonstrations, and draft resistance. Susan became enthusiastically involved in the anti-war movement.

Jean and Howard sent Susan on a tour of Western Europe in the summer of 1965, with her college roommate. The two roommates soon dumped each other and continued the traveling with new boyfriends. President Johnson authorized a huge escalation of the war in Vietnam in July, and Los Angeles was consumed in the Watts Riots. Susan had met new people from all over the world and the United States, and upon return to college in Boston, there didn't seem to be much point in continuing to study "Publication". So, in 1966, she dropped out in the second semester of her senior year and, like so many others her age in that year, she went to California. The year was an experience in growth and independence. On return to Boston, Susan continued the anti-Vietnam activity.

At a rally on Boston Common on October 3, 1967, a handsome young man in an army jacket jokingly asked if she was going to burn her draft card. They went together to Arlington Street Church where Dr. Benjamin Spock, Boston University professor Howard Zinn, and Rev. William Sloane Coffin had gathered a group of young men who actually had draft cards and actually burned them in a collection plate. Henry Billings had returned from US Army service in Saigon a few months before; what he saw there had turned him into an activist against the war. He and Susan were inseparable after that first "pick-up". They spent all their time together through the horrible year of 1968 and the assassinations of Martin Luther King and Robert Kennedy, and married on August 9, 1969.

Susan's sister Christine had been married at eighteen in 1968 to David Switz, a fellow college student in Maine. She dropped out of college to support David, working in a grim electronics factory in Biddeford, ME. She never had an easy life.

Also in 1968, Grace McKee died back in Cortland at the age of 88. Her memory had diminished, but she was healthy in body until she stepped off the front porch of a friend's home, fell and fractured her skull. All the Hamachers but Howard went to the well-attended Cortland funeral, it was the only time Susan ever saw her mother Jean in tears. The relationship Jean had had with her mother Grace was warm and supportive.

Susan and Henry had become engaged earlier in 1968, so, during the funeral week in Cortland, Susan discovered and tried on Grace's beautiful sixty-year-old wedding gown, thinking it would be a nice tribute to her grandmother to wear it. It fit perfectly except for the tiny waist. Susan was not willing to submit to the

Susan & Henry Billings, August 9, 1969

tyranny of the corset, standard practice in 1908, and wore a mini-dress for her own wedding.

John had started at Boston University, dropped out, then went to Bard College in New York, headed west, and spent several years in Colorado, California and Eugene, Oregon, working in construction, often uncommunicative with the family.

Audrey & Henry Billings Sr., August, 1969

Grandmother Grace McKee had left $500 to Susan, who used it to enroll in the charter class of University of Massachusetts/Boston, and finally got a BA in French in 1969, just before her wedding.

Henry Billings came from Somerville, MA, a very different socio-economic background from Susan. In the late 60s, his mother Audrey was a school lunch lady, and father Henry was a hospital custodian. Audrey Wentzel (b. 1910) had immigrated from Nova Scotia as a young adult, worked in factories in Boston and Cambridge, and met Henry Sr. (b. 1900) while boarding at his mother's rooming house in Dorchester.

The Billings family had originally been shipbuilders in Plymouth, England. Richard Billings (b. 1797) left Plymouth in 1823. The family continued the shipwright trade through generations in New Brunswick, Canada, and the state of Maine, ending up in Boston at the turn of the twentieth century where Henry Sr.'s father, Duncan Billings, was a barber. Henry Sr.'s mother was Johanna Maloney, a Catholic who came from Tipperary, Ireland, with her family as a child after the American Civil War.

Our ancestor Henry Billings, was born August 21, 1941, the third child and first boy for Henry and Audrey. He went to Somerville schools, and studied business at University of Massachusetts at Amherst on an ROTC grant, the first of his family to graduate from a four-year college. His older sister Joan had gone to nursing school and had a very successful career at Mass. General Hospital. Of course, the ROTC money obligated Henry to enter active duty, and in 1966, he went to Saigon, Vietnam, as a Second Lieutenant in Intelligence where he wrote reports, played golf, and explored the exotic city far from combat. One of his intelligence reports outlined the illegal US bombing campaign in Cambodia. The report was suppressed.

— CHAPTER 11 —
A New Generation in Vermont

Susan and Henry honeymooned driving across the country in his Volkswagen Beetle (as they left, they learned about the vicious Charles Manson cult murders that had happened in Los Angeles on their wedding day). Reaching San Francisco, Henry called home and learned he had been accepted in a doctoral program back at University of Massachusetts. The couple continued west, spent a romantic week in Hawaii, then drove back to Boston by the southern route through Texas. They settled in a gritty little trailer in South Deerfield, MA. Susan worked at substitute teaching for $25 a day, while Henry attended classes in Amherst. He did all the classwork for the doctorate, but never finished the dissertation. He got a job teaching high school history in Whitingham VT, where Susan worked as a teacher aide, cleaned houses, and waitressed. The couple was following a popular trend of the 1970s, the "back to the earth" movement. It rejected urban and suburban sophistication and turned to a simpler way of life; living in the country, growing one's own food, baking bread. It was a satisfying alternative lifestyle. After three or four years of renting in Jacksonville, VT, they were able to buy a house in Halifax, VT, and have a baby. Parents and grandparents happily welcomed Miles Walker Billings' arrival at Brattleboro Memorial Hospital on his due date of June 26, 1974.

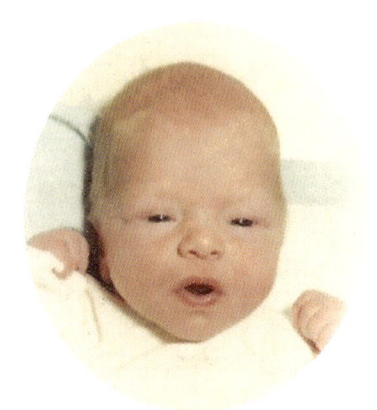

Miles, June, 1974

Miles had the rare distinction of living under three US presidents by the time he was two and a half years old. Richard Nixon resigned in disgrace over the Watergate affair in August of 1974, Vice President Gerald Ford succeeded him, then Ford was defeated in the election of 1976 by Jimmy Carter.

During this time, Henry was teaching and earning extra money coaching girls' softball at Whitingham High. When Miles was nine months old, the couple's second pregnancy began, though Henry was beginning to develop an interest in one of his young softball players, a girl of 14 who lived next door and had done some babysitting for the Billingses.

Jean C. Billings was born December 11, 1975. Her big brother Miles called her Ti-ti, his word for "baby." Susan was ecstatic to have a girl.

Henry's affair with the neighbor girl grew more intense through Jean's first year. He was threatened with a rifle by her father, with losing his job, with divorce, and he finally left the family in the summer of 1976 for a new job in Massachusetts. There was never a question of getting law enforcement or the child protection agency involved. Scandals were hushed up in the mid-70s.

During the spring of 1977, Susan sold the Halifax house, got a divorce (not the first in the family, Chris was divorced twice), and bought a 100-year-old Victorian at 63 Frost Street in Brattleboro which had been partially converted into apartments. She finished the conversion into three units with the help of the US Department of Housing and Urban Development, got work as the manager of the school breakfast program, and raised Miles and Jean in Brattleboro. Her siblings John and Chris each lived at 63 Frost Street for periods while they were going through hard times.

63 Frost Street in Brattleboro

When Miles and Jean both reached elementary school, Susan started work in a grant-supported early childhood program serving low-income parents and their children ages 0 to 3. Under the leadership of the visionary Brattleboro social worker, Judie Jerald, the program expanded manifold into Early Education Services and became a model for other preschool family support programs across the country.

Miles got a very good education at Brattleboro Union High School from 1988 to 1992, starred at ice hockey for the town team, raced bicycles, and made life-long friends. Jean was able to go to Northfield Mt. Hermon Academy (NMH), in Northfield and Gill, Massachusetts, with the help of scholarships and contributions from her father Henry and grandfather Howard. The experience at NMH was life-changing for Jean. She graduated with honors in 1994.

Susan commuted the two hours to Boston and earned a Master's degree in Family Support and Parent Education in 1995 at Wheelock College with the financial help of Early Ed. Services and some private and Vermont state scholarships. The thesis work involved a parent education course at Southeast State Correctional Facility, at the time, a men's medium security prison in Windsor, Vermont.

Early Education Services was a very good career for Susan, personally fulfilling and flexible enough to allow her time with family crises as when 12-year-old Jean broke her left hip skiing in 1988, needing surgery and rehabilitation, and when sister Christine suffered a brain aneurysm in 1996, spent months in the hospital, then was disabled until her painful death in 1997 at the age of 48.

Miles and Jean both graduated from University of Vermont; Miles in 1996 and Jean in 1999. Grandfather Howard and Grandmother Jean (always known as Papa and Noni) attended, along with Uncle John and his wife, Candy Stern (married August, 1992), who had settled in Waterbury Center, VT.

John & Candy's wedding, August, 1992

Christine was too sick to go to Miles' graduation in 1996, and she was gone by Jean's time in 1999. Soon after Miles' graduation, Susan took Miles and Jean on a two-week trip to England.

Miles and Jean each spent some time exploring careers after college. Miles worked in Somerville, Massachusetts for an architect doing computer-assisted design. He enjoyed a winter ski-bumming as a chair lift operator in Jackson Hole, Wyoming with some friends from Brattleboro. He was a manager for the Appalachian Mountain Club at Greenleaf Hut atop Mount Lafayette in New Hampshire's White Mountains. He went to Prague, Czech Republic, to teach English, where Susan was delighted to visit him in February of 2001, making a side trip to a UNESCO World Heritage site, the medieval village of Cesky Krumlov.

During some time off, Miles did more travelling in Eastern Europe, skiing in Austria and visiting Holocaust sites in Poland.

— The Story of An American Family —

Miles & Jean at Shakespeare's birthplace, 1996

Susan in Prague, Charles Bridge in background, 2001

Jean traveled extensively in Asia, teaching English near Pusan, South Korea, then in central Japan in the small city of Shiojiri. Her mother had a wonderful visit there with a side trip to Kyoto in August, 2000.

Jean also enjoyed several weeks in Kuala Lumpur, Malaysia, and returned to the US through Europe. Besides making wonderful friends and absorbing such a different culture, she learned some delicious Asian cooking during that year.

Susan had the freedom to make these exciting trips because, with both children graduated from University of Vermont, and missing and grieving her sister Christine, she determined to leave Brattleboro in 1999, and took a job as a live-in nanny in Berkeley, California at the age of 55. This turned out to be a wonderful career move. She hired a manager for the house in Brattleboro, which was completely rented out. The nanny salary was better than the old job and there were no expenses what with housing, food, and car provided. And, she loved the work. There was only one difficult placement among the four different families she worked for in seven years, and she grew to love the East Bay Area and the many friends she made there.

The attacks of September 11, 2001 happened while Susan was working as a live-in nanny in Berkeley. It was a challenge to reassure her young charges during that difficult day. The family's twelve-year-old daughter thought it was risky to fly the American flag outside the house (as many Americans were moved to do) in case it might make the family the next target. When Susan finally got through to Florida on the clogged phone lines, she asked her 86-year-old father Howard who could have done such a terrible thing. He quickly replied in his characteristic deadpan, "Osama Bin Laden". Of course he was right.

CHAPTER 12
A New Century, Weddings & Babies

During Susan's California nanny years, both Miles and Jean found their partners and got married. Miles met Felicity Smith (b. March 27, 1978) as he was finishing his Master's in Geography in 2002 back at the University of Vermont (UVM). She is a remarkable woman, athletic, brainy, beautiful and humorous. She had just graduated from UVM in ecology studies, number one in her class, after having gone to high school at Brattleboro. She and Miles are four years apart in age, so they never met in high school. Her ethnic background is English; she was brought up in western Massachusetts (very near Blandford) and Guilford, VT. She earned her medical degree at Johns Hopkins in Baltimore, where Miles got his Maryland teaching certificate and supported Felicity and himself working as a private middle school teacher at Indian Creek, near Annapolis. Their Baltimore years were hard work and fun for the couple. They made many friends and did some vacation travelling together to Guatemala and Southeast Asia; Vietnam and Cambodia, where they visited ancient cultural sites and saw chilling reminders of the Vietnam War and the Killing Fields.

Miles and Felicity were married July 31, 2004, on the hilltop above her father Steve's farm in Guilford. The catered reception was in the cleaned-out and polished-up barn that Steve used for his sawmill business.

During the dinner, Felicity's beautiful identical twin sisters, Serenity and Elsie, gave an impromptu trapeze performance (they had previously been employed by Cirque de Soleil) that knocked everyone's socks off. Jean Hamacher, who was now 85 and in good health, attended with Susan. Howard had died at 88, after long decline. He was supported at home by Hospice through a short critical illness, and passed away at their home on December 23, 2003, in Englewood, Florida.

Jean Billings traveled to the Vermont wedding (and served as a bridesmaid) from her new home in Austin, TX, with her chosen man, Rene Sanchez. The couple had met in class at the University of Texas where Jean was in a Master's/PhD program in education. The day after Miles and Felicity's wedding, Rene asked Susan for Jean's hand. The couple officially became engaged in September when Rene astonished Jean with a surprise flight to Seattle for a Red Sox/Mariners game, where he proposed on bended knee in front of thousands. They bought a house in East Austin and married March 19, 2005, under a spreading live oak tree at the Commons Ford Ranch in Austin, followed by dancing to the Western Swing music of the Hot Club of Cowtown.

Rene Sanchez's parents, Anselmo and Edelmira, were each born in Texas to migrant farm worker families. His grandparents were Mexican. His middle name, Omar, reflects the Moorish conquest of Spain in ancient times, and the Spanish colonization of Mexico. Rene (b. June 19, 1970) grew up in Edinburg TX, where his

— Susan Billings —

— The Story of An American Family —

father worked for Hidalgo County. He graduated from Notre Dame University, earned a law degree from Ohio State, and a Master's in Education from University of Texas. He is a brilliant educator, devoted to the concept of public schools in America.

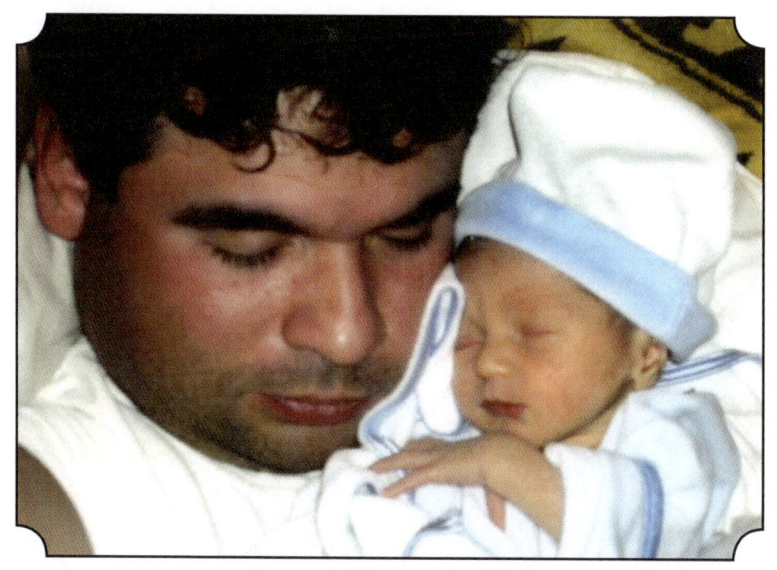

Rene and Cesar snoozing

The Sanchezes' first baby, and Susan's first grandchild, was Cesar Xuauhtemoc, born December 22, 2005, at the Seton Central Hospital in Austin, TX. Named for the great American champion of farm workers' rights, Cesar Chavez, and the last undefeated emperor of the Aztec nation, he was small but healthy at 6 pounds and 1 ounce. Jean had been on bed rest for a few months because of tendencies toward pre-eclampsia, and used her time to work on a grant from Austin ISD, planning a School for Girls which evolved into the Ann Richards School of Austin.

Miles and Felicity came from Baltimore to see the new baby and spend Christmas in Austin in 2005. Nine months later, Keenan Wells Billings was born at Johns Hopkins Hospital on September 12, 2006. He was given his middle name from the Smith family, and "Keenan" was one the new parents just liked.

Felicity was able to count on Miles for tremendous support with the baby while she was in medical school. She graduated from Johns Hopkins in 2007, the family moved back to Boston for her internship at St. Elizabeth's Hospital in Brighton, and Miles began teaching history at Buckingham, Browne & Nichols middle school. When Felicity began her anaesthesiology residence at Brigham and Women's, she and Miles bought a house in Watertown.

In 2006, Jean Hamacher was 86 years old, fairly vigorous in body, but not thinking as well as she once had. Susan had decided it was time to retire from the nanny business, so mother and daughter bought a house on a cul-de-sac in Northeast Austin. Susan and great-grandmother Jean looked after Cesar Mondays, Wednesdays, and Fridays while Jean Sanchez taught special education math at a middle school and Rene was a high school principal. Jean Hamacher's decline was slow but steady. She had several therapies, balance class, a visiting nurse. She enjoyed welcoming Jean and Rene's second child on February 5, 2008, the day of the Super Tuesday primary election which pushed Barack Obama into the lead for the Democratic Party nomination (it was also Mardi Gras). The Sanchezes named their tiny daughter Graciela Susana after Rene's late sister Graciela, Jean's mother Susan, great and great-great grandmothers Grace McKee and Grace Boies Chamberlain.

Eighteen months after Gracie's birth, Susan had an amazing experience for a grandmother; she welcomed two little boys to the family in twenty-four hours. Eli McKee Billings was born to Felicity and Miles on August 3, 2009, at Brigham and Women's Hospital in Boston, where Felicity was now a regularly employed anesthesiologist. Eli's middle name honors his great grandmother Jean McKee Hamacher. Back in Austin, Jean and Rene Sanchez's third baby, Alejandro Anselmo, was born at Seton Hospital on the next day, August 4, 2009. He is called Xander, a name Jean loved, and the middle name, Anselmo, is a tribute to Rene's father.

— Susan Billings —

Cesar at 4 years old

Keenan

Graciela at 1 year old

Xander and Eli, March, 2012,
at 2 years old

Susan and great-grandmother Jean continued to care for the Sanchez children in Austin Monday, Wednesday, and Fridays, a day for each one.

In January of 2010, Jean Hamacher's macular degeneration claimed the last of her useful vision. It was a devastating blow, but she made the best of it by listening to books on tape from the Texas State Library for the Blind, enjoying the antics of the great-grandchildren, and visiting with friends. In the summer of 2011, Rene found a job near Corpus Christi on the Gulf Coast of Texas. The family bought a house together at 209 Southern Street, Corpus Christi, and all four generations moved down to the beach. Jean Hamacher became more and more frail, and had several falls which landed her in the hospital and rehab. Susan's brother John visited often from Vermont, and was with Jean at the Hospice Center in Corpus Christi where she breathed her last, two days after her 93rd birthday, March 18, 2012. Miles, Felicity, and their boys had made plans to visit for her birthday, so all of Jean's living descendants were present. She had a remarkable life.

Jean Hamacher's passing made it possible for Susan and the Sanchez family to move back to the Austin area, where they found a house with room for all at 3105 Richfield Landing in Pflugerville in 2012.

Miles had already finished running the April 15, 2013 Boston Marathon in under three hours, and was recovering at home when two nail-filled pressure cooker bombs exploded near the finish line of the marathon, killing three and injuring hundreds. Several spectators were horribly maimed and required amputations. The following Friday, April 19, Miles, Felicity, and the two little boys were locked down in their Watertown home while police and SWAT teams scoured the immediate neighborhood for the surviving Chechnyan terrorist, Dzhokhar Tsarnaev, who was eventually discovered cowering in a stored boat near Eli's day care. The senseless and brutal attack brought home the risks of Islamic terrorism to the City of Boston where our ancestors began their American experience so hopefully almost 300 years ago.

With a generous inheritance from her mother, Susan had the means to travel to Scotland, Northern Ireland, Massachusetts, and New York to flesh out the family story with pictures and research primary sources in the summer of 2013, though there is always more to be done.

So, Cesar, Keenan, Graciela, Eli, and Alejandro, if you've read this story from start to finish, you know more than most people ever get to know about one part of your family history. You've learned about at least one person from each of fourteen generations going back almost 500 years and ending (up to the present) with you! You come from some remarkably intelligent, brave and hard-working ancestors. They don't seem to let adversity stop them from living the life they want, they forge ahead even when they don't exactly know where they'll end up, and then they make

— The Story of An American Family —

Susan at Dean Castle, Kilmarnock, Scotland

it work. They are thirsty for education and are always able to leave something to the next generation. My hope for you is the same.

For me, researching and writing the story has been a wonderful experience. When I started I knew nothing of our history before my own grandmother, Grace Walrad McKee. Finding our connections to the ferocious Vikings, Scottish nobility, the pious Scotch-Irish linen makers, the courageous freedom-seeking immigrants to America, the pioneers who fought in the American Revolution, and the farmers, industrialists, and businessmen who helped to build the United States—it's all given me a new sense of identity and belonging that I hope each one of you can embrace, too. It's my gift to you.

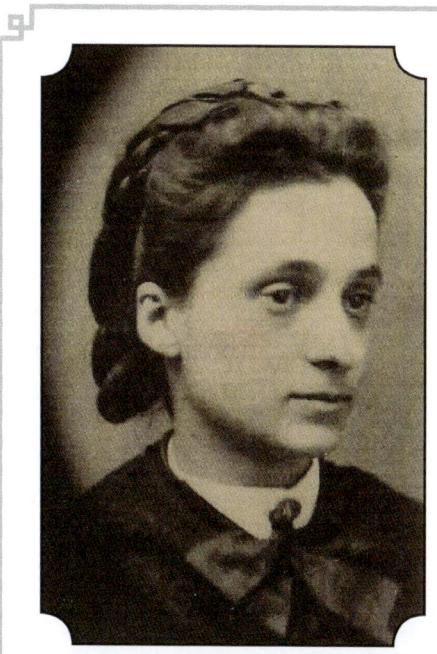

— Family Photo Gallery —

Grace B. Chamberlain, c. 1870

Grace's sister Sarah Chamberlain, C. P. Walrad's first wife

Grace Chamberlain Walrad, c. 1895

Grace Walrad with daughter Grace McKee and grandson Bobby, c. 1912.

— Family Photo Gallery —

Sarah Ann McQuaide Sprague, Frank's grandmother, b. 1826

Nancy Sprague McKee, Frank's mother, 1856–1921

Robert Jackson McKee, Frank's father, 1854–1877

Frank W. McKee at 4 or 5

— Family Photo Gallery —

Frank Wray McKee, at 18, 1877–1923

— Family Photo Gallery —

Infant Gracie, c. 1881

Gracie and sister Anna, c. 1887

Gracie at about 6 years

Gracie, Grace Chamberlain Walrad, Anna, Calvin P. Walrad, c. 1890.

— Family Photo Gallery —

Gracie and Anna in front of 13 Lincoln, Cortland, with their mother and father, another man and cat

— Family Photo Gallery —

Calvin P. Walrad, c. 1908

— Family Photo Gallery —

Gracie and Bobby, 1912

Grace, Bob, Buzz, Cal, 1918

McKee Family, 1923

Gracie McKee, 1928

— Family Photo Gallery —

Grace McKee at about 83

164

— Family Photo Gallery —

Jean at 3 or 4

Jean (l) and friends at the lake, c. 1929

— Family Photo Gallery —

Cal, Buzz, Bobby, Jean and the Essex auto, c. 1924

— Family Photo Gallery —

2nd from left, in uniform, Elwin Hamacher, his wife Mabel, Ethel Hamacher (Howard's mother) with 5-year-old Howard in front. Next to Howard is his grandmother, Martha McTarsney, and several of her other adult children.

Howard at 10 or 11

Howard at about 50

Family Letters

— Family Letters —

Nancy Gibbs Boies's mother, Agness Gibbs writes this letter from Blandford to Homer to inform the family of her husband, Israel's death. The lack of punctuation, differences in spelling, and slips in grammar are all Agness's. The postscript is from Rufus's brother, David Boies. The original letter, written in Agness's hand, is in the Chamberlain Box at the Cortland Historical Society.

Dear Children   March 8, 1818

I once more would inform you that God in his mercy is sparing your affectionate mother and whilst he has afflicted me with the one hand he is in his mercy supporting me with the other My health is considerably impaired though there is no reason to complain. To conclude it is owing to my wounded spirits I am now mourning the loss of my youthfull companion your kind and loving father has bid adieu to this world. He lies beneath the clods of the valley He closed his eyes on the things of time and so on the nineteenth of February He was taken sick on the Fourth of February his disorder of the gravely kind. He had his water drawn twice the third attempt was in vain how much he suffered we cannot tell but he complained very little. He appeared to manifest a great degree of Christian patience and resignation he had a desire to see you all before he died. Instead you so remember your father's memorable and precious words in the last stages of his life, Praise ye the Lord from everlasting unto everlasting remember these words and be faithful that you may injoy and believe the Comfortable [promise] of the resurrection if a man die, shall he not live again. These words was the text preached from at his Funeral sermon as we hope he is yet living in the presence of that God whom he professed to love. Let us unite our voyces and our hearts as humble supplycants at the throne of grace that we may be prepared to meet him and live again pray for yourselves and pray for your mother that she may be supported and comforted under her present troubles.

I sincerely hope this --- will find you enjoying good health. I have a great desire to see you and I hope you will visit Blanford as soon as convenient. your friends and relations are in good health for any we know excepting Silas Gibbs' youngest son . he run a nail in his knee and we hope he will recover so I must subscribe myself your affectionate Mother   Agness Gibbs

Dear Brother and Sister you likely wish to hear respecting my wife's health the sixth of March after suffering more seemingly than human nature could indure she was delivered, and we have one more added to our number a girl she is very low but we hope she will recover

My brother ------Gibbs is ------ to settle in your country---. I wish you to be kind and --- to him in purchasing of ----- we can recommend him as one of the best of members of society of his age

with respect I remain your sincere Brother

David Boies

This money which I enclose in this letter you will receive as a present from your Mother.

— Family Letters —

This letter is from 50-year-old Rufus to his wife Nancy. I can't help wondering if he sold any of his cattle to one of our Hamacher ancestors in this part of Pennsylvania. Coincidentally, I copied the letter at the Cortland Historical Society on July 13, 2013.

July 13, 1828
Dear Friend
   I again sit down to inform you that a Kind Providence has watched over me for 16 Days since I wrote you last and has blest me with a good degree of health for which I have good reason to be thankful for - and I sincerely hope that you and the family have enjoyed the same blessing - . – it is now 32 days since we have left Stephen Russell and I should never known the fatigue of driving a drove of Cattle from Ohio if I had not experienced it. We have had the good fortune to get all of our Cattle along in good order except of which we have sold, we now think that we shall be able to sell at a fair profit, there is a great many speculators meet us every day but have not made an offer that we think will do yet—we are in hopes of selling out in the Course of 7 or 8 days, but we don't calculate to sell below the market yet I feel very anscious to get home or hear from you but cannot I suppose short of 2 weeks. The time seems long since I left my friend. - - - we dismissed Cap't Strong 5 days ago and he returned by way of Meadville We are now 40 miles below Harrisburgh – and 10 miles east of Lancaster and 56 miles from Philadelphia – in the Heart of the Country for Selling Cattle, and they have hay and pastures in Abundance, but they know how to lay out their Money—This from your Affectionate
   Husband
   Rufus Boies
   Nancy Boies
   [inside the folded paper he writes another note]

Israel & Wm I think of you every day and of the haying and Harvesting but I cannot help you any yet. I am in hopes that I shall be able to get home before harvest, we have been traveling through a country where they have been harvesting this 2 weeks past the wheat and rye is all cut in the Country and all the first crop of hay

- - -

I want you to be careful and not work too hard. We have heard of a good many people dying in this part of the Country in the harvest field in consequence of the Heat, week before last.

This from your affectionate

Father   R. Boies

PS please send word to Scott if you have an opportunity that James B is well

Family Obituaries

Martha Hoge Obituary

MARTHA HOGE, daughter of Robert and Letitia Hoge, was born December 17, 1759, in the Juniata Valley. Her parents were natives of South Scotland, coming to America, however, from the province of Ulster, Ireland, where they had sometime resided, in the summer of 1752. They remained in Philadelphia until the year 1754, when they located on a tract of land in the Tuscarora valley, then in Cumberland county, Pennsylvania. In June, 1756, owing to the Indian incursions in the Juniata valley, Mr. Hoge fled with his little family to Carlisle, returning only in the fall of that year. On two other occasions did this early pioneer seek safety in the then principal place of refuge west of the Susquehanna. Martha Hoge married, in the winter of 1777–78, Thomas McKee, who was born in 1749 in County Down, Ireland. He emigrated to Pennsylvania in 1774, and located near the Hoge's in the Juniata valley. At the beginning of the struggle for independence, he entered the service and for a time was under Morgan, in one of the Pennsylvania companies attached to the corps of that brave partisan leader. In the summer of 1777 he served a time in Captain James Power's company of the Second battalion, Cumberland County Associators. Subsequently, when in July, 1778, a call was made for the frontier riflemen to go to the Standing Stone (now Huntingdon), he marched with his neighbors, and in the fall of the same year served as first lieutenant in the Seventh battalion. These really were not the only periods when he was in arms, for all the frontiersmen, being threatened frequently by the wily savages, numerous calls were made for protection in gathering the crops. About the year 1795, Mr. McKee removed to Western Pennsylvania and the year following, settled upon a farm near the present town of Butler, where he died in the year 1814. During the most trying period of our history, his wife vied with the women of her neighborhood in their patriotic endeavors to cheer the hearts of the heroes who were gradually achieving the independence of their country. While the dames of the Quaker City were lavishing their smiles upon the officers of the British army, these backwoods women were spinning and weaving the flax they had raised to make the material to clothe their fathers and brothers, husbands and sons, wintering at Valley Forge. Trying times these were on the frontiers and yet the brave women forgot cares, trials and deprivation, in the thought that the loved ones periling their lives in the common cause, were being ministered to. None were more active in these deeds than the women of the Tuscarora Valley, and their descendants have a heritage grand and ennobling. Mrs. McKee died on the home farm near Butler, Pennsylvania, July 26, 1836, and her remains rest beside those of her patriotic husband.

Martha Hoge was born in Pennsylvania of Scots-Irish parents, and her husband, Thomas, came to Pennsylvania from Northern Ireland as a young adult just before the American Revolution. They were your seven-times grandparents.

— Family Obituaries —

Elizabeth PA Herald dated Friday, November 14, 1884

Captain William Bradford Sprague

Capt. William B. Sprague died at his residence this morning at 6 o'clock, aged 62 years. In his death, West Elizabeth loses one of its leading and most enterprising citizens. Mr. Sprague with his most estimable wife came to Elizabeth some twenty five years ago or more, from Saltburg, Indiana County, where they were married and where both, we believe, had always previously lived. He engaged in business which was continued until the breaking out of the Rebellion, when he went into the field as a Captain of a company of volunteers. He was soon transferred to one of the stationary departments of the Army at Washington where he served through the war and for some years after it closed. Returning to Elizabeth, he opened a drug store, but on the building of the rail-road and the impetus it gave to West Elizabeth he was one of the first to settle on the new portion of it, at the upper end, has since conducted the flourishing drug business there.

He was the father of seven children, four of whom and his wife are still living. The surviving children are Mrs. Mary Smith, and James M. Sprague who make their home together at Pittsburg, Southside, where Mr. Sprague is in business: Mrs. Nan McKee of Glenfield, Pennsylvania; Mrs. George Conrad of Uniontown, Pennsylvania.

In disposition, Mr. Sprague was cheerful and sanguine. He was an affectionate husband and father, and an unfailing friend to all who had claims on his friendship. He was active in every movement for the public good, liberal according to his means, public spirited and a thoroughly good citizen.

Better than all, he was a zealous and earnest Christian, being a member of the Presbyterian Church. The malady with which his life terminated was swelling of the lymphatic glands and his suffering which was intense dates back some months. The funeral will be on Sunday with services at his late residence.

Captain Sprague, the Civil War veteran, and his wife Sarah McQuaide were your fourth great grandparents. They helped their daughter Nancy's children when their father died young.

Pittsburgh Commercial Gazette
Tuesday Morning, July 3, 1877,
Vol XCI, Page 4, Col. 1, Item 6

Sad Case of Drowning

Three young men, Dr. Burns, R. J. McKee and Mr. Glasgow, of the village of Glenfield, on the Fort Wayne road, eight miles below Allegheny City, went into the Ohio to bathe, Saturday evening, about nine o'clock. Having taken their bath, Burns and Glasgow dressed themselves, but Mr. McKee remained in the water, stating that he intended to swim to the opposite shore. They did not see or hear him again, but a man who sat on the river bank stated that he heard McKee call for help. The deceased was a druggist, and was well known and highly esteemed. He leaves a wife and two children. Cannons were fired, on Sunday, in hopes that the body would rise to the surface, but without avail. At last accounts it had not been recovered.

Pittsburgh Commercial Gazette
Wednesday Morning, July 4, 1877, pg. 1,

Body Recovered

The body of John R. McKee, a druggist of Glenfield, who was drowned while bathing on Saturday evening, was found floating in the river at Freedom this morning. His friends were notified, and the remains taken home this afternoon. Mr. McKee leaves a wife and two children.

. . . . A dispatch was received yesterday stating that the body of a man had been found floating in the river at Freedom. As the body was nude, it is supposed to be that of Mr. McKee of Glenfield, who was drowned on Saturday night last while bathing.

— Bibliography —

Beaver [PA] Daily Times. August 18, 1923.

Blodgett, Bertha Eveleth. *Stories of Cortland County*. Cortland, NY: Cortland County Historical Society Publication, Frank Place, editor, 1952.

Boies, Betty E. and Wells, Violet C. *The Descendants of David Boies of Blandford, Massachusetts*. Blandford, MA: R. E. Boies self-published, 1986.

Bolton, Charles Knowles. *Scotch-Irish Pioneers in Ulster and America*. Boston: Bacon and Brown, 1910.

Cortland Standard Daily Newspaper. Cortland, NY: 1908

Gibbs, William H. *Address Delivered before the Literary Association*. Blandford, Massachusetts: Blandford Literary Association, 1850.

Goodwin, H. C. *Pioneer History of Cortland County*. New York: A. B. Burdick & Co., 1859.

Griffin, Patrick. *The People with No Name: Ireland's Ulster Scots, America's Scots Irish, and the Creation of a British Atlantic World 1689–1764*. Princeton, NJ: Princeton University Press, 2001.

Lacy, Brian. *The Siege of Londonderry*. Dublin: Derry City Council, Eason & Son Ltd., 1989.

Lambert, David Allen. *A Guide to Massachusetts Cemeteries*. Boston: New England Historic Genealogical Society, 2009.

Leclerc, Michael J., editor. *Genealogist's Handbook for New England Research*. Boston: New England Historic Genealogical Society, 2012.

Leavitt, Emily Wilder. *The Blair Family of New England*. Boston: D. Clapp & Sons, 1900.

Leyburn, James G. *The Scotch-Irish: A Social History*. Chapel Hill: University of North Carolina Press, 1962.

Martine, Roddy. *Scottish Clan and Family Names*. Edinburgh, Scotland: Bartholomew & Son, 1987.

Norton, Mary Beth. *Liberty's Daughters, The Revolutionary Experience of American Women, 1750–1800*. Ithaca, NY: Cornell University Press, 1980.

Perry, Reverend Arthur Latham. *The Scotch-Irish in New England*. Boston: J. S. Cushing & Co., 1891.

Smith, Henry Perry. *History of Cortland County*. Syracuse, NY: D. Mason & Co., 1885

Sweeney, Martin A. *Lincoln's Gift from Homer, New York; A Painter, an Editor and a Detective*. Jefferson, NC: McFarland & Company, 2011.

Tabraham, Chris. *The History of Scotland*. Grantown-on-Spey, Moray, Scotland: Colin Baxter Photography Ltd., 2010.

The Purple Pennant, newsletter. *In Fond Memory*. Cortland, NY: Cortland High School, January 18, 1951.

Walrad, Grace Boies Chamberlain. Personal family papers. Circa 1890.

Webb, James. *Born Fighting: How the Scots-Irish Shaped America*. New York: Broadway Books, 2004.

Wood, Sumner Gilbert. *Taverns and Turnpikes of Blandford 1733–833*. Blandford, MA: self-published, 1908.

Made in the USA
Charleston, SC
22 April 2015